Getting the Best Deal for Your Money

Getting
the Best Deal for
Your Money

Jean McGlone

Published by Consumers' Association
and Hodder & Stoughton

Which? Books are commissioned and researched by
The Association for Consumer Research and published by
Consumers' Association, 2 Marylebone Road, NW1 4DX and
Hodder & Stoughton, 47 Bedford Square, London WC1B 3DP

First edition September 1989

British Library Cataloguing in Publication Data
McGlone, Jean
  Getting the best deal for your money.
  1. Personal finance
  2. Title II. Consumers' Association
  332.054

ISBN 0 340 49197 3

Edited by Jonquil Lowe
Verification assistant Judith Samson
Typographic design by Tim Higgins
Cover illustration and cartoons by John Holder

Photoset in Linotron Plantin by Paston Press, Loddon, Norfolk

Printed and bound in Great Britain by
BPCC Hazell Books Ltd
Member of BPCC Ltd
Aylesbury, Bucks, England

Contents

Introduction

Personal finance is big business. There are plenty of firms keen to gain your custom: they spend vast sums on advertising, sales forces and wooing advisers who can provide clients.

Marketing is an essential part of today's finance industry and it generally serves the consumer well by conveying information about the products and services on offer. But, by its nature, marketing is biased – it aims to win you over to a particular product or service. You need to keep a good lookout to spot the best deal. Independent advisers help, but you should always bear in mind that advice is seldom really free, and there are stresses on the advisers which might sway them to recommend one type of product, or one company, rather than another.

Forewarned is forearmed. This book alerts you to potential problems and to smart moves you can make to get the best deal. With over 100 TIPs and WARNINGs, sections on financial self-defence and copious 'points to note', this book trains you to navigate safely the choppy waters of personal finance.

If, nevertheless, things do go wrong, the book outlines your legal rights, and gives full details of how to make an effective complaint. It points out your options in seeking redress and tells you when there's a possibility of compensation. Throughout, the addresses and phone numbers you're likely to need are supplied.

The book covers a wide stretch of financial areas, giving you the information and advice that you need to put the marketing claims into perspective. It takes you from mortgages to credit cards, bank charges to cashless shopping, house insurance to car insurance, life cover to paying medical bills, National Savings investments to shares, doorstep salesmen to seeking out advice.

In short, it is the essential navigation chart for consumers who don't necessarily want the products and services which make the most noise, but want to seek out the best deal for their money.

1

Selling styles

There was a time when a fool and his money were
soon parted; now it happens to everybody. Adlai Stevenson

A very obvious change in the financial scene of recent times has been the
way in which its various products and services are marketed to the
general public. No longer do you have to go along to your local bank or
building society with your best suit on to ask for a loan, nor are you short
of advice when seeking a suitable home for your savings. Today the
financial world comes a-wooing whether you're an existing customer or
not. Everything from loans to life insurance and unit trusts is offered,
using the same techniques that sell washing powder or chocolate bars:
cartoon characters promote share issues on TV; glossy leaflets extolling
the virtues of credit cards pop through the letterbox; and eye-catching
advertisements for investments appear in all kinds of publications. High
profile financial marketing is here to stay.

How can you cut through this mass of information to make sure that
you end up with the right deal? The best defence against getting a bad
deal is to be armed with some knowledge about the techniques used in
the financial world, recognising the good points and the pitfalls, being
aware of the controls that are set by current legislation and voluntary
codes, and knowing what you can do if you think the rules have been
infringed to your detriment.

Printed advertisements

Advertising in the UK is controlled by a patchwork of complementary
and, sometimes, overlapping rules; some are voluntary codes, others are
statutory regulations. Central to this patchwork is the British Code of
Advertising Practice which comes under the aegis of the Advertising

Standards Authority. The Code covers all printed advertisements whether, for example, in newspapers, magazines, on hoardings, posted through your door, or in leaflets in shops. It lays down general rules which advertisements must follow in order to meet the central tenet that they be legal, decent, honest and truthful. It includes a section applying to financial advertisements which deals with a number of more specific points. The Code is voluntarily adopted by the advertising industry, but it's generally effective, because sanctions, such as adverse publicity or denying future advertising space, can be brought to bear on any offender.

The main drawback of the British Code of Advertising Practice is that it's couched in fairly general terms which don't always go far enough. Two areas which have traditionally caused difficulties are investments and loans. These are now covered by statutory controls – under the Financial Services Act 1986 and the Consumer Credit Act 1974, respectively. (Regulations under both these Acts go beyond printed advertisements and cover most other forms of advertising as well.) Where other industries have encountered problems they have adopted their own codes to supplement the provisions of the British Code of Advertising Practice – for example, this has happened with banks and building societies, particularly in relation to advertising their interest rates on savings accounts.

The general rules applying to *all* financial advertisements are:

- advertisements must be balanced, accurate and not likely to be misunderstood by those at whom they are targeted, including anyone who can't be expected to have any special understanding of the subject matter
- anything stated to be fact must be based on evidence available at the time of making, or publishing, the statement
- all promises and statements must be accurate and not misleading.

WARNING *There can be widely differing views about what is misleading. For example, an advertisement for a type of deposit savings account claimed '… your* capital is completely safe – the cash you put in is the cash you get back.' *While it was true that the amount of ££s invested couldn't decrease, the buying power could be seriously eroded by inflation. Just five per cent a year inflation over a ten-year period would reduce the buying power of each £1,000 to a little over £610, and the real value of income earned by the deposit would similarly fall. However, the British Code of Advertising*

Practice doesn't outlaw the expression 'completely safe' in this context, and legislation which would outlaw it doesn't apply to this form of savings.

Advertisements for investments

The British Code of Advertising Practice rules applying to investment advertisements are fairly general. Much more detailed and stringent rules were introduced under the Financial Services Act. The most important of these are outlined below.

WARNING
The Financial Services Act (and hence its rules governing advertising) doesn't apply to deposit-type investments, such as bank and building society accounts, National Savings Bank accounts, and deposit-type pension plans.

Who, what and where An advertisement must include the name of the advertiser and, in most cases, the name of the regulating body which oversees the company's activities (see p. 156). The nature of the investment concerned must be clear. If full details of the investment aren't given, the advertisement must say from where you can get full written details. If the act of applying for details could trigger a visit or phone call from a salesman, the advertisement must make that clear too.

Closing date 'Offer closes by 30 June' used to be a familiar sort of phrase which might well be perfectly genuine: for example, issues of new shares have a set closing date, or an imminent change in the law might affect a particular product. But, in many cases, the provision of a closing date was simply marketing hype.

The new rules say that only if an investment is actually available for a limited time, in limited quantities, or on special terms for a limited period, is the inclusion of a closing date permissible.

Tax-free 'Up to £11,791 tax-free cash!' exclaimed the leaflet for a life insurance savings plan. The words 'tax-free' once featured largely in such advertisements. There's nothing in the new rules to say that they shouldn't still, but certain provisos are included so that claims will be less misleading than some may have been in the past.

The description can be applied only to those investments which are genuinely tax-free, such as National Savings Certificates or friendly society bonds; with these, no tax is payable either by you or by the organisation running the investment. On the other hand, the proceeds of some types of life insurance may be tax-free in your hands but the insurance company itself will already have paid, or set aside amounts to cover, income tax, corporation tax and capital gains tax. You can't reclaim the tax paid by the company. In such instances, the words 'tax-free' may still be used but the fact that the proceeds are payable out of a fund from which tax on income and gains has already been paid must also be stated and given equal prominence – in other words, the information can't be tucked away in tiny print where it might easily be missed.

WARNING *Do not confuse the words* 'income paid free of tax' *with* 'tax-free'. *The former means that income from the investment is handed over to you before any tax has been paid – for example, as with National Savings Income Bonds or British Government stocks (except when bought through the Post Office – see p. 128). But these proceeds count as taxable income and you may have to pay some tax depending on your particular circumstances.*

Performance claims '22 per cent a year – unit price growth since 1976' and similar phrases used to be common enough claims. A more colourful alternative was a graph showing clearly the staggering growth of the fund. This technique invites you to think that future growth will be as good. But a great deal of research – much of it in universities and business schools both here and in the US – strongly concludes that past performance is not a reliable guide to the future. Performance claims can still be used in advertisements, but they must carry a warning that past performance is not necessarily a guide to future performance. And the new rules limit the ways in which past performance can be quoted so that advertisers can't create a misleading impression by deliberately picking on a period of exceptional growth. Even so, you'd be wise to pay little heed to performance claims.

WARNING *The rules do not set out any specific form of wording, leaving the way open for cloudy variations. For example, an advertisement can legitimately say:* 'Though past performance cannot guarantee the future, the figures speak for themselves.' *Translation:* 'We've got to warn you about investment performance in general, but don't worry about ours!'

Projections 'Invest just £25 per month now, collect £16,145 in 15 years' time' is an example of another well-used technique. Research into investment performance has failed to find any reliable methods of predicting future growth – what will happen to your investment is anyone's guess. Under the new rules, projections are still allowed and are commonly used in the sale of life insurance and pensions. But now projections must be given using standard growth rates, so the advertiser can't make his product more appealing simply by basing forecasts on optimistic assumptions about future growth. Projections must also be based on standard charges. So companies selling the same sort of products will quote the same projected returns – you can't use projections to compare different companies' products. If projections are made, they must be accompanied by a statement about the effects of inflation to show how inflation eats into the buying power of your investment.

TIP *Projections tell you very little and shouldn't influence your choice of investment or company. Unfortunately, the statement about inflation is long and difficult to use – ask the company, salesman or your adviser to do the sums for you.*

Risk warnings Advertisements must also warn you if the value of your investment can fluctuate – for example, as with unit trusts and unit-linked life insurance. If you can't afford to lose any of your capital, or if you might need money back in a hurry (perhaps when unit prices are low), you should avoid investments carrying this warning.

In advertisements which invite you to take up an offer – for example, by filling in a coupon included as part of the advertisement – other warnings may be required. If a deduction for charges or expenses would fall heavily in the early years of the investment, this must be made clear. This could be the case with, for example, many regular premium life insurance policies. Investments with this warning would not be the place for money that you couldn't leave invested for the long term. You must also be warned if the return on the investment depends on what profits are made and how they are distributed – as with with-profits life insurance policies. In some circumstances, there might also be a warning that an investment is unsuitable for inexperienced investors – if, despite the warning, you're still attracted, you'd be wise to get the help of a professional adviser.

Commendation The word 'commendation' is used to describe any statement in an advertisement made by someone commending or endorsing a product. Under the rules, any quotation or statement used in this way must fairly represent the views of the person to whom they are attributed. If the person is an employee or associate of the company – in other words someone who has a clear vested interest in the product and whose commendation might reasonably be thought to be partial – the advertisement must say so.

WARNING

The rules say nothing about the use of a well-known person to add impact and credibility to a product being advertised, and who might by implication, if not in spoken word, seem to be commending the investment. But bear in mind that usually they'll also have a vested interest in the product because they are being paid a fee.

Advertisements for deposits

Advertising of deposit savings accounts, such as those offered by building societies and banks (including finance houses) is covered by the British Code of Advertising Practice and supplemented by a voluntary code under the auspices of the Bank of England and the Registry of Friendly Societies. The main areas covered by the Code are outlined below. Deposit-based personal pension plans are also to be covered by additional rules (covering aspects such as projection of possible benefits) – regulations under the Social Security Act 1986 were expected to come into force in 1989, but had not been announced at the time this book went to press.

Interest rates An advertisement does not have to quote interest rates. But, if it does, then it must show either the 'gross rate' – the rate before tax has been deducted – or the 'net rate' – the rate you get after the equivalent of basic rate tax has been paid. (Banks, building societies and most similar organisations have an arrangement with the taxman whereby they hand over tax at a special 'composite rate' before paying you or crediting you with interest. If you're a basic rate taxpayer there's no more tax to pay. Higher rate taxpayers have extra tax to pay. Non-taxpayers can't reclaim the tax already deducted.)

The net rate can be accompanied by something called the 'gross equivalent rate'. This can be for either basic rate or higher rate taxpayers, and tells you how much before-tax income you'd have needed to earn elsewhere in order to have been left with the quoted net rate after meeting your tax bill. (The gross equivalent rate will be higher than the gross rate because basic rate tax is higher than the composite rate tax paid by the organisation.)

The advertisement can also quote the gross or net 'compounded annual rate' (CAR). This takes account of when you are paid, or credited with, the interest.

TIP *The compounded annual rate tells you the true return you're getting and is the rate you can compare with the returns available on other deposits or other investments.*

Withdrawal terms An advertisement should tell you the normal withdrawal terms for the account being advertised – for example, any notice period, or interest penalties. If there's always a penalty on withdrawal, then phrases such as 'instant access' and 'immediate withdrawal' mustn't be placed next to the interest rate, if shown, because in practice you'll never achieve the quoted return.

WARNING *Advertisements for deposit savings accounts don't have to mention any limits on immediate withdrawals imposed by your branch of the bank, or building society – for example, a maximum of £300 cash per day – and can use phrases such as 'instant access' even when such limits apply. (Though one Trading Standards Department has stated that this might contravene the Trade Descriptions Act 1968, this view has not so far been put to the test.) A leaflet available at the branch should include this information or at least warn you that there may be a limit. So make sure you get and read all relevant literature before you open an account.*

Advertisements for loans and credit

'Low-cost finance – special deals', 'preferential, quick and trouble-free finance', 'quick loans – any purpose'. Nowadays, there seems no end to the offers of loans and credit. There are special loans for members of motoring organisations, for credit card holders, special deals for doctors, and credit for students. If you can't yourself think of a reason for taking out a loan, the advertisements will help you with suggestions of second cars, holidays in the sun, or the kitchen of your dreams. And if you're already struggling to cope with a backlog of debts, there are plenty of advertisements encouraging you to take out a single loan for

CASE HISTORY

A member of a motoring organisation was sent an invitation by its financial services arm to take out a personal loan. The letter said that the organisation had negotiated with a particular bank in order to provide its members exclusively with preferential, quick and trouble-free finance facilities. The tables accompanying the mailshot explained that the rate of interest would be fixed at the time the loan was taken out and a particular Annual Percentage Rate (APR) was quoted.

The member was surprised that not only was the interest rate much higher than that currently being offered by many High Street banks – in some cases over 5 per cent higher – but the loan package also seemed very similar and therefore not at all exclusive to members of the organisation.

Moral: If you're tempted by a special offer, don't automatically assume that you're getting a good deal. Check that you can't get the same, similar – or even better – goods or services elsewhere at a better price.

'paying off all your store card bills' or to 'put all your eggs in one basket' and 'even have cash to spare'.

The majority of loan advertisements come within the ambit of the Consumer Credit Act 1974. The Act doesn't cover advertisements aimed at companies and doesn't cover advertisements for loans which will always exceed £15,000 unless they are secured loans (see p. 36). The definition of advertisement is very wide, covering not just printed advertisements of all kinds but even the patter of a salesman as well as radio and TV commercials, displays in shops, and so on.

Advertisements are divided into three types, with different rules applying to each:

- simple advertisements. These give just the name of the advertiser and an indication that they're in the business of giving loans or credit. They're the sort of advertisements that might appear on a business card or a complimentary book of matches, say

- intermediate advertisements. These must give a certain amount of information – for example, name of the advertiser, phone number and/or address for getting a written quotation, conditions attached to the loan such as the need for security or insurance, or a requirement to open an account from which repayments are to be made. Where the credit is for a fixed amount to buy particular goods, the cash price of the goods must be shown for comparison and also the cost of the loan expressed as an Annual Percentage Rate (APR – see p. 37). The advertiser can choose to include certain other information as well to give a better picture of what's being offered
- full advertisements. These must include a great deal of information, including name and address of advertiser, the APR, any conditions such as the need for security, any restrictions on who can take out the loan or credit, the amount of any advance payments, the amount and frequency of subsequent payments, and in most cases, the total number of repayments, the total amount payable under the deal, and the price if you paid cash.

Secured loans 'Secured' means that the lender has a right to certain of your assets if you fail to repay the loan as agreed. Commonly, such loans are secured against your home. The rate of interest charged on secured loans is usually lower than for other loans, because the lender runs a lower risk of being out of pocket.

Secured loans don't just include a bank or building society mortgage to buy your home; many credit firms and credit brokers advertise these loans for any purpose whatsoever. And, with the huge rises in house prices during much of the 1980s, banks and other lenders have marketed 'equity release' schemes which let you borrow money against the security of the difference between the market value of your home and the mortgage still to be paid off. Despite the rather grand name, equity release schemes are essentially little different from other forms of secured lending. The important thing to remember about any secured loan is that, if you default, you could lose your home.

WARNING *The law requires advertisements to state the need for any security. But such statements are often hidden away in the tiniest of print, and the words used don't necessarily make the situation clear. Research by the National Consumer Council in 1987 found that an alarming number of people thought the*

word 'secured' *was an indication of the stability of the lending organisation rather than a description of the type of loan. In some advertisements,* 'Homeowners only' *is prominently displayed, but it's not clear that's because their home will be needed as security. New regulations under the Consumer Credit Act are due to be introduced. These will require advertisements for secured loans to carry a* 'health warning' *saying* 'Your home may be at risk if you don't keep up payments' *or similar words. In the meantime, always check carefully whether a lender requires security – especially if the loan looks relatively cheap.*

Direct mail

An increasingly popular way of seeking customers for financial products and services is to send advertisements through the post. The technique relies heavily on the use of lists – usually computer-generated – of people grouped by, say, where they live, shares they've purchased, and so on. Using a list lets the provider of the product or service closely target his advertising to the people most likely to buy.

Extra rules   Direct mail is another form of printed advertisement and as such is covered by the British Code of Advertising Practice, as well as the other codes and laws already looked at above. But direct mail poses particular problems: as it's sent to a restricted group of people it's more difficult to keep a check on the advertisements, and most direct mail advertisements are inviting you to take up an offer there and then, often employing the help of special gifts and inducements to this end. So there is a Direct Mail Services Standards Board which monitors direct mail on behalf of the Advertising Standards Authority, and the Code includes extra rules covering such areas as offers of free gifts.

WARNING *Pick a financial product on its own merits; don't be swayed by the offer of a free gift. If the product or service is better than, or at least as good as, others of its type, then you can look on the gift as a real perk. But if you buy the product or service without regard to its own worth or the alternatives available, your* 'free' *gift could turn out to be very expensive. Note that the rules require that a free gift should arrive within 28 days. If it arrives damaged or broken, you are entitled to a replacement.*

Mailing lists   There are two types of mailing lists. *'Compiled lists'* are made up, often by specialist companies, from freely available information, such as that contained in electoral registers, street or phone directories, share registers, and so on. *'Response lists'* are compiled within an organisation either for internal use or for rent or sale to other organisations. You get onto a response list as a result of buying something or showing an interest in a product – for example, you might subscribe to a particular magazine, or have taken out cover with a motoring organisation. It's good practice for an organisation with whom you're doing business to let you know that your details might be put on such a list and to give you the opportunity to decline, but at present not all organisations take this approach.

TIP *If you ask, an organisation must tell you if you're on a computerised list that they have. For a fee you're entitled to a written copy of the information held. You can, without charge, have incorrect data about you corrected. These rights, which you have under the Data Protection Act 1984, apply only to automatically processed data held about you, and not to manually compiled and stored lists.*

Compiling, renting and buying or selling lists is big business and there are brokers who specialise in it. Checks are made on the organisations or people using such lists but occasionally these are not very rigorous.

Sending you unsolicited direct mail advertisements is perfectly legal, but you might find it irritating. Many direct mail advertisers now belong to the Mailing Preference Service; if you want to reduce the amount of direct mail that you receive you can ask the service to have your name removed from its members' mailing lists. You can also use the Service to specify the types of direct mail that you would like to continue getting or even ask to be added to more mailing lists. You can contact the Service, or get an information leaflet about it, by writing to:

Mailing Preference Service
Freepost 22, London W1E 7EZ

WARNING *If direct mail which you wish to cancel, using the Mailing Preference Service, is wrongly addressed make sure you give the Service the incorrect version of your address as well as the correct version. Otherwise, the computer won't pick out all the mail to be stopped.*

TIP *If you're getting unwanted mail from an organisation which doesn't belong to the Mailing Preference Service, you should write to the organisation direct asking them to remove you from their list. Most organisations will comply, as they have no wish to pay for advertising that they know won't work.*

Small print

With some advertisements you'd need a magnifying glass to read all the details, so it can be all too easy to miss something important. There are some regulations regarding the relative prominence given to specific information. For example, the Consumer Credit Act requires that loan advertisements display the 'true' interest rate (Annual Percentage Rate – APR – see p. 37) more prominently than any other interest rate and at least as prominently as various statements describing the loan. 'Prominence' encompasses not just the size of type, but other techniques also, such as use of colour, position and repetition. The Financial Services Act includes some similar rules – for example, information about the risks inherent in an investment can't be shown in type that's smaller than that used for the main text of the advertisement. But such rules are patchy, and there's no general requirement for all parts of all advertisements to be easily legible, nor any official guidance on how ease of reading could be achieved.

Advertisements on television and radio

Advertisements broadcast on television and radio must comply with a code of practice set up and administered by the Independent Broadcasting Authority (IBA). Statutory requirements, such as those of the Financial Services Act and Consumer Credit Act, also apply.

The IBA code has a section dealing specially with financial advertising. An advertisement will normally be accepted only if it relates to a business which is governed by statute law or by some other form of proper regulation – for example, banking business can usually be advertised only by banks within the meaning of the Banking Act 1987, general insurance by companies conducting business under the Insurance Companies Act 1982 and investments by those authorised under the Financial Services Act 1986.

Some regulations regarding the relative prominence of information – such as those under the Consumer Credit Act (see p. 16) – apply to broadcast advertisements as well as printed ones. In the context of television, or radio, advertisements could contravene such rules if, for example, information were not given additional emphasis or shown in larger type on the screen

Advertisements which reach your television or radio are fairly unlikely to be breaking the rules because they are all vetted on behalf of the IBA before being cleared for transmission.

Salespeople

You might prefer to sort out your financial business in your own home, especially if you have the assistance of a salesperson whom you know and have done business with before. But a selling technique which you'll probably come up against from time to time is 'cold calling' – the uninvited visit or phone call from someone you don't know. For many people, having an uninvited salesperson in the living room is an unwelcome and even intimidating experience. Even an uninvited and unwanted phone call can be difficult to handle if you're not prepared in the last resort to be rude.

In general, financial matters are complex and you shouldn't be harried or hurried into making a deal. Unfortunately, cold calling of financial products isn't outlawed though it is restricted, and there are rules and codes of conduct aimed at preventing the worst abuses. But, because cold calling is a one-to-one technique witnessed normally by just the salesperson and customer, it's difficult for an outside authority to make absolutely sure that the rules are being followed. So it makes sense for you to be on your guard and prepared to complain if you're unhappy about a cold call made on you.

Doorstep selling

As far as investments go, this form of cold calling used to be restricted to life insurance. Sadly, the Financial Services Act extended this technique to unit trusts and many types of personal pension plan. Other types of investment can't be sold in this way, nor can most loans or credit.

WARNING *Loans related to buying specific goods can be sold door-to-door, so a salesperson could legitimately call at your home and try to sell you a satellite dish for your television, or double glazing, say, on hire purchase or credit.*

21

WARNING *Where a loan isn't connected to buying something specific, a salesperson can't visit your home unless they've previously got your permission in writing to do so. Be careful that you don't unwittingly give your written permission when you sign a form for something else – for example, a request for further details or a quotation.*

If you don't want to talk to a salesperson who appears on your doorstep, you should politely but firmly say just that and then close the door. But if you're at least interested to hear what they have to say then it will help if you understand something of the techniques they are using and the rights that you have. The points below will guide you through a visit from a salesperson arriving on the doorstep to sell you investments.

Identifying the salesperson   At the start of a visit, the salesperson must reveal their name to you and the name of the company they're working for – they should give you their business card. They must also make clear whether they're selling the products of just one company, or whether they're an independent adviser who'll cover the whole market for each type of product that they sell. (There's no halfway house – an investment salesperson can't be representing two or three companies, say.) Most doorstep salespeople fall into the first category and are representing, or are exclusively associated with, one company only.

WARNING *Watch out for the 'disguised' salesperson who tells you that they are doing market research into the investment habits of the neighbourhood, or completing a survey for a financial magazine. This practice is called 'sugging' – selling under the guise of market research. It's illegal for an investment salesperson to use this technique, and if you come across it, you should report the salesperson to their company and to the relevant regulating organisation (see Chapter 8).*

The salesperson must at the outset state the reason for their visit and find out whether or not you want them to carry on. If you do, they must then describe the products they have to sell.

The sales pitch   An investment salesperson is legally required to give you the best advice they can (for more about this, see p. 142). They must not make any statements which are untrue or exaggerated, nor must

CASE HISTORY

Mr K received a letter from a finance house asking for his help in a market survey on consumer credit. If he filled in a questionnaire he would be sent a modest number of holiday vouchers. He was promised a rather larger number of holiday vouchers if he decided to avail himself of the finance house's advice to restructure his loans. When Mr K looked at the questionnaire he found that it asked for some detailed personal information, such as his income, the nature and amounts of any loans, and his attitude to secured loans and re-mortgages. At the end it asked if a consultant could call round to show Mr K how his monthly outgoings could be considerably reduced if he restructured his loans.

Mr K suspected that he was the target of some 'sugging' – selling under the guise of market research. When the finance house was approached, they said that they had intended to use the results for market research, not primarily for selling, but if someone had agreed to a visit from a consultant, they would of course pursue the custom. In the opinion of the Advertising Standards Authority, though, the letter was primarily a sales promotion because it was offering an incentive to use the loan advice.

they make light of any drawbacks concerning their wares. If the products they have to offer are really unsuitable for you, the salesperson should admit this. And they must respect your right to end the visit at any time. But there's little point in ignoring the fact that they are there in the hope of making a sale. And the salesperson has a whole armoury of ploys to help them gain your trust – and business. These are some of the techniques you may encounter. The salesperson's position at the door will have been worked out in advance. Too close and too eager to come in might appear threatening. Wiping the feet on your doormat is designed to trigger you to invite them in. Once inside, a man may take off his coat but not his jacket – that should seem neither too formal nor too casual. They'll probably ask where to sit rather than risk taking your favourite chair.

The salesperson is required by law to find out enough about you to enable them to assess your needs and match you to suitable products. But sometimes, identifying a genuine need tips over into encouraging you to invent 'needs' you don't really have – a new car, luxury yacht or exotic holiday, perhaps. The salesperson may try to get you to tell them the minimum you can save regularly, rather than telling you the minimum a savings contract requires – this way they avoid the risk of putting you off with a figure that's too high or settling at a figure that's lower than you'd have been prepared to invest.

The dotted line The salesperson may be very keen to sign you up before they'll leave. Don't be pressured. If you don't want the product, or if you want time to think it over and to look at alternatives, say so. Don't be swayed by talk of deadlines, or unrepeatable terms – a hasty financial decision can end up costing you more than a delayed one. But if you do sign during the visit and then want to change your mind, you can. You must be sent a 'cancellation notice' following the visit. This will set out the details of the contract and tell you that you have 14 days (starting from the time you received the notice) in which to cancel the deal without penalty.

TIP *Buying from someone who turns up on your doorstep is unlikely to give you the best deal for your money. The salesperson will often be representing just one company, so they'll be unable to seek out the best deal from the whole market.*

Selling by telephone

This type of investment selling is also restricted to life insurance, unit trusts and many types of personal pension. Loans can also be sold in this way.

A loan salesperson needs your *written* permission to visit your home – they can't just phone you up and arrange to meet. So, perversely, you may find a cold phone call being used to persuade you to take out a loan there and then over the phone. But the deal can't be completed this way. You'll have to sign a properly drawn up agreement. The salesperson may invite you to their premises to sign – and if you do, you'll then be bound by the agreement. But if the document is posted for you to sign at home, with most loans, you'll have a 'cooling-off period'. The lender must send back to you a copy of the signed agreement and you have up until the fifth day after you receive this copy to cancel the deal if you wish.

WARNING *Beware of agreeing to a loan over the phone. You've no way of being sure of the identity of the caller. But they'll usually need personal information which you wouldn't normally make freely available, such as details of your income and your bank.*

An investment salesperson will usually be more interested in trying to get you to agree to a personal interview rather than doing business there and then. The sort of tactics you might encounter include:

You: I'm too busy.
Salesperson: Yes, I do appreciate you're an awfully busy person and I'm quite willing to come at any time that would suit you. I could make it early in the evening – say, before you've really settled down – or after dinner, if you prefer, to have a chance to relax a bit.
You: I always rely on my bank manager for advice on insurance matters – so really there's no point you coming round.
Salesperson: Delighted to hear that – shows you're just the sort of person my company's products are suited to. It can't possibly do any

harm to take a look at what we've got to offer – you might just find we can manage a much better deal. Could I put you down for seven on Friday? I'll be in your area anyway then.

TIP *If you find cold phone calls irritating, put the phone down. Don't say you're too busy to talk – that might suggest you'd be willing to on another occasion. Just say you're not interested and hang up.*

Self-defence

No laws can stamp out all abuse. The really determined fraudster or con-man will always survive. You can't expect total protection from sharp practices, so you should adopt a few self-defence techniques when the salesperson calls:

- if you're not interested, say so at once and close the door or hang up the phone
- if you *are* interested in the product in general terms but doubt your ability to resist the sales spiel, ask the salesperson to give or send you some literature and their business card so that you can get in touch when you've had time to consider the product. If they won't agree to your suggestion, close the door or hang up
- if you're interested and want to know more, invite the salesperson in or agree to meet. But try to remember that this is someone who is basically after your money, not a friend you've invited round. Many people feel that someone in the living-room always deserves to be treated as a guest; but if the salesperson is too persistent, you'll have to be inhospitable
- bear in mind that salespeople are trained to be socially adept. If you remind yourself that a lot of what they say and how they behave has been carefully rehearsed, you won't feel so bad if you decline to do business
- even if the products are genuinely the best on the market, bear in mind that it doesn't make them good value for money if you don't actually need them, you have them already, or you can't afford them
- remember that if you are persuaded to agree to a deal, you have a cooling-off period, in most cases, during which you can change your mind.

Classroom commercials

Commercial sponsorship of educational material for schools is a growth industry. More and more teachers are using leaflets and worksheets which have been prepared by commercial organisations, including financial ones. General money management is a favourite topic, but in explaining the various ways of handling money, the difference between impartial information and partial advertising can be very slight.

Consumer groups have voiced concern about the possibility of such erstwhile advertising material being used in schools, and an E C consumer committee has suggested that the content of sponsored material might be controlled to avoid the possibility of disguised advertising.

If you're worried that your child may be being taught about personal finance in an imbalanced or less than partial way, discuss it with the teachers – perhaps at a parent-teacher association meeting. It might be possible to correct any bias with leaflets from other sources.

Complaints

If you think a printed advertisement is unfair, misleading or otherwise unacceptable, write detailing your complaint and where and when you saw the advertisement (enclosing a copy if possible) to:

Advertising Standards Authority (ASA)
Brook House, 2–16 Torrington Place, London WC1E 7HN

Complaints about television or radio advertisements should be sent to:

Independent Broadcasting Authority (IBA)
70 Brompton Road, London SW3 1EY

If the advertisement is breaking the law, the ASA or IBA will pass the complaint on to the relevant authority. If you're already aware that the law has been broken, or if your complaint concerns forms of advertising other than the printed or broadcast word, send your complaint to your local Trading Standards Department (look in the phone book under Trading Standards Department and this will direct you to the relevant local authority address and number). Complaints about investment advertising covered by the Financial Services Act should be sent to the relevant self-regulating body (see Chapter 8).

2

The basics of borrowing

Let us live in as small a circle as we will, we are either debtors or creditors before we have had time to look around. Goethe

Lending is big business, and loans and credit are readily available as 'an easy, reliable way to bring just about anything you want within your reach' as one lender put it.

But borrowing should be approached with common sense: getting the money is often the easy part; paying it back can prove more difficult. Most lenders make careful checks before they agree to a loan, and turn down applicants who they think are unsuitable. For example, the major credit card companies say they turn down over a third of all applicants. But some lenders are not so responsible and, ultimately, you are the one who must decide whether or not borrowing is sensible given your personal situation. And bear in mind that circumstances can change – losing a job, a marriage breakdown, a long illness, or a sharp and prolonged rise in interest rates are all events which could turn manageable borrowing into a debt crisis. But used with care, loans and credit are useful tools in your financial planning.

Basic rules

- If you can't meet your current spending (shopping, mortgage payments, fuel bills, and so on) out of your available income, *don't borrow*. Trying to repay the loan will only exacerbate the situation. Instead look at ways of cutting back on spending, or adding to your income.

- Before you take out a loan, check that you can meet the repayments. Work out your income and normal spending precisely. Look at your take-home pay (in other words, after taking off tax and other deductions) and don't include payments which can't be relied upon, such as overtime and bonuses.
- Don't borrow up to the hilt – try to leave yourself with some uncommitted money so that you can cope with the unexpected. This is especially important if the interest you're paying on the loan could rise.
- Always shop around for the best deal. There are nearly 75,000 lenders legally operating in the UK, so you have plenty of choice.
- Get proper quotations for the loans that you're interested in. Compare the terms, especially the true cost of each loan (see p. 37) and the need for any security (see p. 35), charges if you want to pay off the loan early (see p. 35) and so on.
- Think carefully before committing yourself to a long-term loan. Do you know that your circumstances might change during the term – for example, are you due to retire, are you hoping to start a family? If so, will you still be able to afford the repayments? Do you want some protection against unforeseen changes, such as redundancy or long-term illness? If so, you could take out loan insurance which will make the repayments for you in some of these circumstances, though such insurance is fairly costly, and may not suit your circumstances – for example, if you're self-employed. If you have dependants, make sure that you have enough life insurance to repay the loan as well as cover the rest of their needs if you die.
- If you are in desperate financial straits or already badly in debt, don't borrow more to pay off your existing loans. Get help from a debt counsellor (see p. 40).

Are you creditworthy?

Lenders don't make profits out of bad debts, so it's in their interests as much as yours to check that potential borrowers will be able to repay their loans. Many lenders go to great lengths to do this, using techniques such as credit scoring and subscribing to credit reference agencies.

Credit scoring

This is a statistical technique, used by most lenders, for automatically assessing whether you're likely to be a good or a bad credit risk. It's

similar to the way insurers try to put people into different risk categories for car or life insurance.

Credit scoring systems are usually computer models developed by specialist firms and sold to lenders. The systems use data about loans that have been made in the past to work out which characteristics of the borrowers tend to be attributes of good borrowers and which of bad ones. The characteristics are given a score; different lenders use different systems, but generally a high score means the characteristic is associated with a good lending risk and a low score with a bad risk. When you apply for a loan, you'll be asked for various personal details. These will be scored in the same way and added together to give a total. If your total score is above a certain level, you'll automatically be granted credit or given the loan. If it's below another level, you'll automatically be refused. In between, there's a grey area where the lender will have to investigate further before deciding whether or not to lend to you.

Nowadays, credit scoring systems are quite complex and virtually all include information provided by credit reference agencies (see p. 32) which might account for the largest part of your 'score'. But the following very simplified example shows how a system might work:

A Simplified Credit Scoring System

Employment		Bank account	
Unemployed	0	Yes	4
Unskilled	1	No	0
Semi-skilled	2		
Skilled	4	**Marital status**	
Professional	5	Married	4
Self-employed	3	Single/widowed	1
		Divorced/separated	0
Length of time in your present			
employment		**Age**	
Less than a year	1	Under 18	0
1–3 years	2	18–29	2
More than 3 years	4	30–49	6
		50–59	4
Housing status		60+	1
Owner	5		
Unfurnished tenant	2		
Furnished tenant	1		
Length of time in your present			
home			
Over 3 years	4		
1–3 years	2		
Less than a year	0		

The credit scoring system will also take account of other factors such as, the geographical area in which you live, your income, and possibly the number of credit cards held and other loans outstanding. A report from a credit reference agency will be an important item.

It would be unusual for any one item making up the credit score to cause a rejection of your loan application – more likely, it would be because of a combination of items plus a bad report from a credit reference agency. For example, a 24-year-old in an unskilled job living in an inner city rented flat who got into difficulties repaying a loan four years ago, while a student, might find their loan application rejected out of hand. But different lenders use different scoring systems, so even if you've been rejected by one lender, you might be accepted by another.

A good credit scoring system should reduce the risk of your application being turned down on purely arbitrary grounds, and it should help to speed up the handling of applications so you may get a loan faster. But the problem with statistical systems such as these is that they tell the lender only about averages. You may share a number of characteristics with people who are in a bad debt category but you might still be a very sound borrower. For example, the 24-year-old above might be about to start a new and much better paid job with excellent career prospects.

TIP *Volunteer extra information to a lender if you think that it might improve your chances of getting a loan. If you're still turned down, ask the company why. They aren't obliged to tell you anything, except – if you ask – whether they obtained a report from a credit reference agency.*

Credit reference agencies

The majority of lenders consult a credit reference agency when you apply for a loan. These agencies collect and collate information about people's lending habits from a variety of sources – for example, bankruptcy records and lists of unsatisfied County Court judgments. Lenders who use the agencies also provide information about their own borrowers' repayment histories. This includes details of loan defaults, and late or missed payments – so-called 'black' information. Most lenders also provide the agencies with 'white' information – details about loans which you did pay off within the agreed terms – and this can help to show that you are a good credit risk. Banks don't provide 'white' information – under your implied contract with your bank, it would be a breach of confidentiality (see p. 87) for the bank to disclose this information without your specific consent. The position is different with 'black' information because, by defaulting on a loan, you are deemed to have already broken the contract with the bank.

You can find out what information, if any, a credit reference agency holds about you by writing to them, or phoning, for an enquiry form. You complete and return this, enclosing a fee of £1. Three large agencies dominate the market:

Infolink Limited
CCA Department, Regency House, 38 Whitworth Street, Manchester M60 1QH
Tel: 061-236 8511

CCN Systems Limited
Legal and Consumer Affairs Department, Talbot House, Talbot Street,
Nottingham NG1 5HF
Tel: 0602 410888

Westcot Data
10 Union Street, Glasgow G1 3QX
Tel: 041-248 6789

If you've been told that you were turned down by a lender as a result
of a credit reference agency's report, the lender must give you the name
and address of the agency, so that you can check your file if you wish.
(Most lenders will automatically provide you with the necessary enquiry
form.) The Consumer Credit Act 1974 gives you the right to request the
agency to correct any errors on your file. The corrected file must be sent
by the agency to all the lenders who've consulted it within the last six
months.

TIP *A credit reference agency has 28 days to respond to your request
for a correction to your file. If they don't reply or if they refuse
to alter the file, you're entitled by law to write your own correction note
which the agency must add to your file (unless they intend to ask the
Director General of Fair Trading to arbitrate in the matter).*

What sort of loan?

Before you approach particular lenders for a quote, you should work out
what sort of loan would best suit your purpose and situation. The main
points to think about are considered below.

What is the loan for?

Some loans are more suitable for some purposes than others. Chapter 3
gives details of all the main types of loan, but here are a few general
pointers. Bank overdrafts (p. 58) and credit cards (p. 62) are often good
choices for short-term borrowing to pay household bills, buy a new hi-fi
or to pay for a holiday. Some shops offer their own credit schemes
(p. 64) – these can be expensive, but 'interest-free' credit is usually a
good deal as long as you can't buy the same goods more cheaply in
another shop. Insurance company loans (p. 66) and bank ordinary loans

(p. 59) are excellent for longer-term purposes, such as buying a car or paying for an annual season ticket – some employers offer free or low cost loans for this sort of thing as well. For home improvements, extending your mortgage (p. 53) or taking out a second one (p. 54) are likely to be good routes. But check out a number of loan sources before you commit yourself to one.

How much do you want to borrow?

Some lenders will give you the full amount you ask for. But others may want you to meet part of the cost yourself depending on what you want to use the loan for and on your particular financial situation. For example, a bank making a personal loan for the purchase of a new car might want you to pay at least a fifth of the cost yourself. You'd need to borrow elsewhere if you were unwilling to do this. In some cases, if you pay part of the cost yourself, you might be able to get the lender to agree to a lower interest rate.

How long do you want to borrow for?

Other things being equal, your monthly repayments will be lower on a longer-term loan than on a short one. But over the whole period the long-term loan will usually cost more than the shorter-term one. You might consider it worth tightening your belt a little so that you can afford the higher repayments on the shorter-term loan. This could be a wise move because longer-term loans tend to be a bit more risky – it's difficult to foresee your circumstances far ahead when you might not be able to manage the loan so easily as now. If you do choose the longer-term option, consider taking out loan insurance (see p. 29). With some loans, there's a maximum term for the loan depending on what you want it for – for example, a bank personal loan for the purchase of a second-hand car might have a maximum term of two years.

Fixed or variable interest?

With some loans, such as personal loans (p. 60) and some shop credit schemes (p. 64), the interest rate is fixed at the time you take out the loan. You know exactly how much you'll have to repay and when. This can help you plan your budgeting, but if interest rates fall you could be stuck with an expensive loan. Other loans, such as overdrafts (p. 58) and mortgages (p. 44) have a variable interest rate which yo-yos up and down with interest rates generally. Sometimes you can put off – at least for a while – increasing your payments in line with the increase in the interest rate but that does, of course, add to the amount of money that you owe.

Will you have to provide security?

You can usually borrow more cheaply and for longer if you're prepared to put up some kind of security – usually your home, or some kinds of life insurance policies. If you fail to keep up the loan repayments, the lender can use the security or the proceeds of its sale to get back what you owe. You should never take out a secured loan unless you are sure that you can repay it within the specified time.

TIP *Though a secured loan will be cheaper than an unsecured loan from the same source, check that you can't get a cheaper unsecured loan from another lender.*

WARNING *If a loan is secured on your home and you fail to keep up the repayments, you could lose your home. In 1988, building societies alone forced the sale of some 20,000 homes because of failure to keep up mortgage repayments.*

Note The legal system for secured loans is different in Scotland and, as a result, charges associated with secured loans are much higher than elsewhere.

Will you want to pay off early?

As long as the agreement for the loan is 'regulated' (see p. 36) under the Consumer Credit Act, you have the right to pay off any loan whenever you like. The lender has the right to be compensated for the interest they've lost because of the early repayment. But they can't charge you the full amount of interest that you would have paid had you kept the loan going – you have the right to a rebate of part of it. The Consumer Credit Act lays down a formula which must be used to calculate the amount of the rebate that you get. Some lenders make an 'early redemption' charge if you pay off a secured loan before the end of its original term.

Guarantors

If you're having difficulty getting a loan, a lender might be more willing if you can find someone to act as guarantor. This means that in the last resort the guarantor will pay back what you owe if you can't. But before going down this course you should consider whether it would be better to do without the loan. Be wary of acting as a guarantor yourself – you could be left out of pocket. And make sure that you cancel in writing your agreement to act as guarantor once the loan has been repaid – otherwise you could find yourself liable for other loans subsequently taken out by the same borrower.

Are you entitled to any special concessions?

If, say, you're a student you might be able to get a loan from a High Street bank at a special low interest rate, simply because they're trying to attract new business and the student of today represents the executive of tomorrow. Some lenders offer special loans to doctors, new graduates, members of motoring organisations, holders of existing credit cards or loans, and so on. Always check that these really are 'special' for you and that you can't get a better deal elsewhere. You might be offered prizes as an inducement to take out a loan. You should never let such inducements tempt you to take out one loan rather than another unless the loan is in any case the one best suited to your needs.

Comparing credit deals

The task of comparing different loan and credit deals is not simple though it's considerably easier now than it was before regulations under the Consumer Credit Act 1974 were introduced. The Act sets out rules concerning most aspects of the business of lending, including the information you are to be given before you take out a loan.

When does the Act apply?

The Consumer Credit Act applies to loans up to £15,000 made to individuals (which includes the self-employed) but not companies. Large parts of the rules apply only to 'regulated' loans – these are all loans falling within the scope of the Act except those which are specifically exempted from being regulated. The most important exemptions are most mortgages that you take out to buy your home, charge cards and most other very short-term loans connected to the purchase of specific goods. Unsecured loans up to £50 are exempted from large parts of the Consumer Credit Act, too, even if they count as regulated loans.

Getting a quote

When you enquire about a loan or credit deal, the lender or shop must normally give you a written quotation covering certain details about the loan if it's a regulated one, or one secured on your home. But a quote doesn't have to be given if the goods or services you're interested in cost no more than £50, or full details of the loan are prominently displayed in the shop when you visit it, or in certain other circumstances.

The quotation must include information such as the name and address of the lender, the cash price of the goods or services you want, the amount of any deposit that you have to put down, the number, frequency and amount of the repayments, the need for any security, the total amount that you'll have to pay over the period of the loan, and the total cost of the loan expressed as an Annual Percentage Rate (APR – see below), and whether the interest rate or any other costs are variable. There must also be a note saying how long the quote is valid.

If the lender can't give you a quote because, say, they haven't got enough information about you or your needs, they can either write to you for the details they need, or they can supply you with a quote based on assumptions which they must make clear.

TIP *Unfortunately, shops in particular are sometimes very lax about producing proper quotes despite the requirements of the law. Don't be fobbed off by counter staff; insist on seeing the manager or someone else who can give you the proper details.*

Annual Percentage Rate (APR)

The APR is a way of expressing the true cost of a loan taking account of not just the amount of interest to be paid, but also *when* the payments are to be made and the impact of any other charges you have to bear as a result of taking out the loan – for example, arrangement fees. The APR is given as a percentage figure and looks just like an ordinary interest rate but must be identified as the APR and must be given more prominence than any other rate included in the quotation.

Here is an example of how a 'flat rate' (often quoted by lenders) compares with the true rate – APR. Suppose you borrow £100 which must be repaid in four equal instalments made over a year. You're charged £10 interest which means that you repay £110 in total and the flat rate will be 10 per cent. But in reality, you're borrowing the full £100 only for the first three months. You then make the first repayment of £27.50 (£25 capital and £2.50 interest), so you're borrowing only £75 during the next three months, £50 in the next and just £25 in the last quarter of the year. So the £10 interest is really being paid on a loan which is lower than £100 for most of the period and this represents a true cost to you of 16 per cent. This figure is the APR. The flat rate makes the loan look deceptively cheap.

Working out APRs is complicated but you don't need to be able to do this yourself – even most lenders use pre-calculated tables. What it's important to know is that you can use the APR as a yardstick to compare the cost of different loans. The APR should be used in conjunction with other information about the loan to decide which is the best method of lending for you.

TIP *If the APR on one loan is higher than the APR on another, this means that the first loan is the more expensive. Use the APR to make your decision about which lenders to approach for further details. (Always approach a few, if you can.) Request a quotation from each, so that you have all the facts you need to make your final decision.*

WARNING *Not all lenders have to quote APRs – for example, those offering overdrafts don't have too, and often don't.*

Read the small print

Before you finally lay hands on your loan, you'll be asked to sign a credit agreement which sets out the terms and conditions. The agreement is a legal contract, so read it carefully before you sign. This may be hard work – the Consumer Credit Act requires that the information be 'readily legible', but it doesn't require that it be readily intelligible. If you are unsure about any of the terms or conditions, ask the lender to explain what they mean. If you're still unhappy, get advice from your local Citizens Advice Bureau (address in the phone book).

The agreement is effective only when both you and the lender have signed the agreement. Usually you'll sign first. You must be given a copy of the document you've signed. There might then be quite a delay before the lender signs (while your creditworthiness is checked, say). You must be sent a further copy of the agreement within seven days of the lender signing it too. So, with most loans, you must be supplied with two copies of the agreement. The lender won't be able to enforce it unless they have followed the procedures correctly.

Changing your mind

If you sign the agreement for a regulated loan at the lender's offices or in the shop where you're buying goods or services, you can't change your mind and subsequently back out of the deal.

But if you sign elsewhere – say, you take the agreement home to study, or it's posted to you, or an agent brings it to your home – you have a 'cooling-off' period in which you do have a chance to change your mind. When you're sent the second copy of the agreement it must be accompanied by a separate note telling you about your right to cancel. You have *five* days, starting with the day after you received the note, within which to give your written notice that you wish to cancel the deal. You're deemed to have given the notice as soon as you've put it in the post (regardless of how long it takes to reach the lender) but you'd be wise to have some proof of posting – use registered post or get someone to witness you putting it in the box.

The cooling-off period is a particularly welcome safeguard where you have entered perhaps rather hastily into a loan agreement made, say, over the phone, or through a door-to-door salesperson who was selling double glazing, fitted kitchens or the like.

WARNING *The cooling-off period doesn't apply to secured loans. This is a quirk of the law – secured loans must be notified to the Land Registry, which can't cope with subsequent cancellations of the arrangement. Instead, the Consumer Credit Act requires that you must be given at least seven days to study a copy of the agreement for a secured regulated loan and think about the deal before you can sign it – if you're not given this pause the agreement can't be enforced. Neither the lender nor anyone else involved in arranging the deal should contact you during that seven days. The copy must contain a note headed* 'Your right to withdraw' *telling you what to do if you don't want to proceed with the deal, though in practice you need do nothing at all – simply don't sign anything.*

CASE HISTORY

A twenty-year-old shop assistant living with her parents was earning under £100 per week. In under a year she ran up debts of nearly £2,000 with three mail order firms, two banks and a credit card company. She decided to borrow part of that sum from a finance company to help pay off her existing debts, but at an APR of well over 300 per cent she was clearly making her problems worse.

In the end she went to her local Citizens Advice Bureau, who took up her case with the local Trading Standards Office. They advised that the APR set by the finance house wasn't likely to be considered extortionate by the courts, given the girl's financial status and the fact that the loan was unsecured. The CAB asked her creditors to let her pay off her debts in small instalments, and all but the finance company agreed. She did eventually pay off the debt but wished she had gone to the CAB earlier.

Getting into debt

Always keep a check on your borrowing and on your changing circumstances. If you start to get into difficulties with your borrowing, act fast – it's easier to solve a small debt problem than a larger one. Here are some guidelines on what – and what not – to do.

Tell lenders what's happening

Don't just miss payments. Many lenders will try to sort out a new arrangement to help you over a temporary crisis – for example, you might be able to make just interest-only payments on your mortgage, or spread your borrowing over a slightly longer period.

Get professional help

Money Advice Centres and many Citizens Advice Bureaux employ professional debt counsellors who are experienced in dealing with debts of all kinds. They will give you advice, help you re-organise your finances and contact lenders on your behalf. The address and phone number of your local CAB is in the phone book. You can also get help and advice about dealing with debts from:

Housing Debtline
318 Summer Lane, Birmingham B19 3RL
Tel: 021-359 8501

Don't borrow more to pay off your debts

You'll have seen newspaper advertisements suggesting that you take out just one loan to pay off all your others – and even leave you cash to spare (see p. 15). Don't be tempted. Such loans either have very high interest rates or they would be secured against your home. If you're already having problems with your borrowing, these loans are likely to make the situation worse, and you certainly shouldn't add to your problems by putting your home at risk.

Protection and complaints

Licensing

Under the Consumer Credit Act, lenders making loans to individuals up to the value of £15,000 must be licensed. It's a criminal offence for them to carry on their business if they're not. There are a few exceptions such as local authorities. Also, lenders making loans of less than £30 don't, at present, need a licence, though the government is reviewing this. Other people and businesses, involved in lending, such as credit brokers, debt collectors, credit reference agencies and debt counsellors must also be licensed at present, though the government has proposed that in future they might not have to be.

Licences are issued by the Office of Fair Trading and, in theory, they should be granted only to fit and proper concerns. In practice, the OFT doesn't have the resources to check applicants thoroughly and only 898 licences have been refused or subsequently revoked over the last ten years out of some 218,000 applications.

Local Trading Standards Departments are responsible for monitoring the licence holders and making sure that they are complying with the Consumer Credit Act.

But there are lenders who flout the law and get away with it. The situation is made worse because people who are in debt to these lenders are often unwilling to give evidence against them – usually because they fear the lender will tell their family or employer about the debts or the lender has made other threats.

If you come across a money lender who's trading without a licence, inform your local Trading Standards Department or Consumer Protection Department – if you look under that entry in the phone book you'll be redirected to your appropriate local authority entry which will give the address and phone number of the Department.

Protection against excessively high interest rates

Under the Consumer Credit Act, a lender shouldn't charge an 'extortionate' amount for loans or credit, but the Act doesn't define 'extortionate' – it's up to the courts to decide, in individual cases. They'll take into account the particular circumstances of the loan – the creditworthiness of the borrower, the prevailing interest rate, whether the borrower was pressurised in any way, and so on.

All loans – even if they're over the £15,000 limit – can be reviewed in this way. But only the borrower can ask for such a review – not the local Trading Standards Department or a debt counsellor, say. You can ask for the review during court proceedings started by a lender to whom you owe money, but you can also take the initiative yourself and ask the court to review the interest rate you're paying on a loan which isn't in default. If the court decides that the rate of interest is extortionate, it has very wide powers to alter the loan agreement. It's a good idea to get legal advice before going to court.

WARNING

The court's view of what's extortionate and what's not can be an unpleasant shock. For example, in one case, an APR of 57.3 per cent was being charged, but the judge ruled that the deal was not extortionate because the loan was for a very short period of time, was fairly risky from the lender's point of view, was arranged at very short notice with few checks being made, and the judge was convinced that the borrower was well aware of the circumstances when he took out the loan.

Complaints

If you have a complaint about, say, the way your loan is being handled, charges you're being asked to pay, and so on, first take your complaint to the lender who issued the loan – insist on seeing the manager if other staff can't help. If you're not happy with their response and they are part of a larger organisation, take your complaint to the head office – the address will usually be on any letter you've had or can be provided by your branch. If you don't know whom to contact there, you could phone up and ask, or you could address your letter to the Complaints Manager. Also, libraries keep company directories which will give you the name of the top executives of the company together with its head office address – so you could write to one of them if you have no other contact.

If you still don't get a satisfactory response, you might be able to take your complaint further. If the lender is a bank, or Access or Barclaycard, you could try contacting the Banking Ombudsman (see p. 163). If the lender is a building society, you could contact the Building Societies Ombudsman (see p. 164). If the lender belongs to one of the lenders' trade associations which have a voluntary code of conduct for members, you could contact them as follows:

Finance Houses Association
18 Upper Grosvenor Street, London W1X 9PB
Tel: 01-491 2783

Consumer Credit Trade Association
Tennyson House, 159–163 Great Portland Street, London W1N 5FD
Tel: 01-636 7564

Consumer Credit Association (UK)
Queens House, Queens Road, Chester CH1 3BQ
Tel: 0244 312044

National Consumer Credit Federation
98/100 Holme Lane, Sheffield S6 4JW
Tel: 0742 348101

If you think that your complaint may involve a breach of the Consumer Credit Act, contact your local Trading Standards Department (address from the phone book, as above).

3

Ways of borrowing

The difficulty in life is the choice. George Moore

There are literally dozens of different ways to borrow. Mortgages, credit cards and bank loans are perhaps the most familiar, though even with these the number of variations can be surprising, and they are certainly not the only choices. The following pages outline the main types of borrowing, suggesting when they are suitable, and tell you which types to avoid altogether.

Borrowing can be grouped into three broad categories: loans to help you buy a home, other ways of borrowing against property, and other types of loans and credit.

Mortgages

Finding a mortgage
Buying your own home is likely to be one of the biggest purchases you'll ever make, and most people borrow to make it possible. Ten years ago, your mortgage would nearly always have come from a building society but today only around 60 per cent come from building societies; the rest are from High Street banks and other new lenders, such as foreign banks, insurance companies and specialist mortgage companies. And gone are the days when you had to be an existing saver in order to qualify for a loan. The mortgage market is very competitive and it pays to shop around for the mortgage which suits you best.

TIP *If you're getting a mortgage for the first time, ask two or three lenders what they can offer you before you make a choice. If you've had a mortgage before, don't feel you have to stay with your previous lender – see what other lenders can offer.*

WARNING *Many estate agents have links with lenders. But remember that what you gain in* convenience might be outweighed by the lender or loan not being the most suitable for you.

The range of different mortgages has increased too, so that you now have a surprisingly wide choice. But not all lenders promote the full range, and unless you ask you might not be offered some of the more unusual types of mortgage. Lenders offering to arrange insurance or pension policies linked to your mortgage are covered by the Financial Services Act, and must either be selling the policies of just one company or must give you completely independent advice – and they must make clear which they are doing. If they are independent, they must offer you the policy which is best for you.

WARNING *Under new rules proposed by the Securities and Investments Board, independent advisers will be allowed to survey the market at intervals and pick the best policy to suit a particular group of customers – for example, those seeking endowment mortgages. This means that the policy chosen might not in fact be the best for you personally.*

WARNING *If you go to an insurance company for a mortgage, they'll probably insist that you take out one of their endowment or pension policies to go with the mortgage. Many other lenders have ties with insurance companies and may be keen for you to link your mortgage to an endowment policy because they earn commission on the sale of the policy. Consider other types of mortgage too and only choose a pension- or endowment-linked mortgage if that's really best for you.*

TIP *If you have trouble finding a mortgage – for example, you need an especially large loan, or for an unusual property, or you can't find the type of mortgage that you want – you could go to a mortgage broker. They survey what's on the market and shop around for you – though some are tied to just a few lenders and won't check the whole market. Some mortgage brokers even have their own tailor-made schemes. But check how much the broker will charge you – one or two per cent of the value of the loan is common though this may be reduced by the amount of any commission they get for arranging an insurance or pension policy to go* *with the mortgage. If, within six months, you don't take up a mortgage arranged by the broker, or no mortgage offer is made, the broker is entitled to a fee of only £3 – as long as you wanted the mortgage to provide a home for yourself or a relative. You may have paid a fee in advance; if so, you can reclaim it, less the £3. Mortgage brokers advertise in the press, or you can find one through a trade organisation, such as:*

Corporation of Insurance and Financial Advisers
6–7 Leapale Road, Guildford, Surrey GU1 4JX
Tel: 0483 39121

Another change to the mortgage market in recent years is the increase in the amount you can usually borrow. Nowadays, it's common for lenders to set a maximum of three (sometimes three- and-a-half) times your salary if you're single, and between two-and-a-quarter and three times the higher salary plus once the lower salary for a couple. And you may be able to get a loan for the full value of your home without having to provide part yourself (though the value will be decided by the surveyor and may be less than the asking price, and you'll still need to pay the fees and expenses involved in buying the property).

Borrowing the maximum possible mortgage is fine as long as you can afford the repayments, but don't borrow up to the hilt – if interest rates rise you could be in difficulties. And remember that your income could fall unexpectedly – if you're made redundant, or suffer a lengthy illness, say. You could consider taking out insurance which would cover your mortgage payments if you were made redundant or fell ill, though such insurance is fairly pricey.

WARNING *If you're unable to keep up your mortgage repayments, you could lose your home (see p. 35), and, if house prices have fallen, you might still owe money on the mortgage.*

The amount you can borrow varies from one lender to another, so shop around. Other factors you should take into account are the cost of the mortgage, the quality of service that you get, and the small print of the mortgage documents – watch out in particular for 'early redemption charges' which are a special charge of perhaps three months' interest if you decide to pay off the mortgage within the first few years. Do make sure that you read all the documents you are sent, and get an explanation of anything you're unsure about.

TIP *If you're a first-time buyer, you might qualify for the government's Homeloan scheme. If you register under the scheme and save for at least two years with one of the building societies or banks (including the National Savings Bank) in the scheme, you can get a tax-free cash bonus of up to £110, and a loan of £600 which is interest-free for the first five years. You must be buying a home under a certain value which varies according to the part of the country you're buying in. In order to take advantage of the scheme, you must register before 31 March 1990. For full details, see the leaflet* Homeloan – special help for first time homebuyers *available in many building societies and banks.*

TIP *You're not stuck with the mortgage you took out when you bought your home. If you find it's expensive compared with mortgages from other lenders, or if you're not happy with the standard of service you're getting, consider switching to another lender. But weigh up the costs of switching which will include valuation and legal fees – and possibly an early redemption charge (see p. 35) – against the benefits, and remember that a lender whose mortgages are relatively cheap now might not stay cheap.*

Mortgage tax relief

Interest on the first £30,000 of loans taken out to buy your only or main home qualifies for income tax relief. Before August 1988, each single person, or each married couple, had their own £30,000 limit – so joint buyers other than married couples could get relief on loans much greater than £30,000. But from 1 August 1988, the £30,000 limit has applied to *each property* regardless of the number of buyers.

TIP *If you're joint home owners who aren't married and have a mortgage of more than £30,000 taken out before August 1988, be wary of replacing your existing mortgage – you'll get tax relief on only £30,000 of a new mortgage.*

Most people now get tax relief through MIRAS (Mortgage Interest Relief at Source). This means that you deduct basic rate tax from your interest before you pay it. Under this scheme, you can get this tax relief whether or not you're a taxpayer. Higher rate taxpayers can claim extra relief from their tax office.

WARNING
Some lenders are not in the MIRAS scheme – avoid these if you're a non-taxpayer. (Non-taxpayers can't claim mortgage interest relief through their tax office.)

Repayment mortgages

How they work Your monthly payments are part repayment of the amount you've borrowed (the capital) and part interest. In the early years, most of the payment is interest. In later years more of your money goes towards paying off the capital.

There are two types of repayment mortgage depending on how the tax relief is worked out. With a 'level repayment' mortgage, your payments (after tax relief) stay the same throughout the mortgage except when interest rates or the basic tax rate changes. An 'increasing repayment' mortgage is harder to find; with this, your repayments are lower in the early years, but rise every year.

Points to note If you have dependants, you'll need a 'mortgage protection policy'. This is a type of life insurance (see p. 104) which will pay off the mortgage if you die during the mortgage term.

Verdict Repayment mortgages are a good choice for most people, because they are very flexible. If, for example, interest rates rise to such an extent that you can't cope with the payments, the lender may agree to extend the mortgage term or to let you make interest-only payments for a while. Cost compares well with other types of mortgage.

Endowment mortgages

How they work You don't pay off any of the loan until the end of the mortgage term. Your monthly payments are made up solely of interest. In addition, you pay premiums for an investment-type life insurance policy which will mature at the end of the mortgage term and be used to pay off the loan.

By far the most common mortgage of this type is the 'low-cost endowment' mortgage. 'Low cost' means that, in order to keep premiums down, the insurance company *guarantees* to pay only a certain amount when the policy matures, but on top of this there will be bonuses added. It's hoped that the guaranteed sum plus the bonuses will be enough to pay off the mortgage – and perhaps leave a bit over for you as well.

A variation on the usual low-cost endowment mortgage is a unit-linked one. With this, you don't get bonuses. Instead the amount the policy pays out on maturity depends on the value of units in a fund of investments to which the policy is linked. This type of endowment mortgage is more risky than the others because the price of the units can fall as well as rise.

Other types of endowment mortgage are 'with profits' – which guarantees to provide enough to pay off the mortgage and you get the full benefit of the bonuses added; and 'non profit' – which guarantees to provide exactly the amount needed to pay off the mortgage with nothing to spare. Both these types of endowment mortgage are expensive compared with the 'low cost' route and are rarely used.

Points to note With all endowment mortgages, the insurance element will repay the loan in full if you die before the end of the mortgage term, so there's no need to take out separate insurance to protect your dependants. If you move your mortgage, you might find the new lender is unwilling to accept your existing endowment policy and might insist that you take out a different one. But an endowment policy is a poor short-term investment and if you cash it in early you could get back very little (even less than you've paid in premiums), so you'd be wise to carry on the endowment policy even if it's no longer linked to your mortgage or, better still, find a lender who will accept your existing policy.

WARNING *Don't be too impressed by quotations saying how much your policy will eventually be worth. Quotations are covered by the Financial Services Act 1986 and must use standard assumptions about investment returns and charges, so all companies give the same quotes for the same type of policy. And bear in mind that inflation will erode the proceeds of the policy, so that the handsome-sounding surplus you might get once the mortgage is paid off might not be worth a great deal in 25 years' time. Equally, it's possible – though unlikely – that the proceeds of a low-cost endowment policy might not be enough to repay the whole mortgage, but any shortfall is likely to be very small after taking inflation into account.*

Verdict Depending on the policy you choose and the level of interest rates, payments for a low-cost endowment mortgage can work out lower than for a repayment mortgage. But endowment mortgages are less flexible than repayment mortgages if you run into problems keeping up the payments. And the insurance element of an endowment mortgage could be expensive if you have a history of poor health. The built-in life cover is useful if you have dependants.

Pension mortgages

How they work These work in a similar way to endowment mortgages, but instead of linking your mortgage to an insurance policy, you link it to a pension plan instead. Your monthly payments comprise just interest. At the same time, you make contributions to a pension plan. At the retirement date under the plan, you take part of the proceeds as a tax-free lump sum which you then use to pay off your mortgage. Pension plans are a very efficient way of saving because your contributions to the pension plan qualify for full income tax relief and the invested contributions grow tax-free.

Points to note If you have dependants, you'll need to take out a mortgage protection policy (see p. 46) to pay off the mortgage in the event of your dying before retirement. Paying off your mortgage should not be your primary reason for taking out the pension plan – if the taxman suspects that it is, the tax benefits might be withdrawn. There are a few schemes linking an employer's pension scheme to a mortgage, but most schemes use personal pension plans. Pension mortgages are even more inflexible than endowment mortgages because you can't cash them in before retirement.

Verdict Pension mortgages can be useful for higher rate taxpayers but, for others, the monthly payments tend to be higher than for repayment or low-cost endowment mortgages. Make sure that paying off your mortgage won't leave you short of money in retirement.

Unit trust mortgages

How they work These are fairly new and in some ways similar to unit-linked low-cost endowment mortgages (see p. 49). You don't link your mortgage to an insurance policy; instead you invest in a unit trust (see p. 132) which is cashed in at the end of the mortgage term and used to repay the loan. During the mortgage term, your monthly payments are used to pay the interest on the mortgage.

Points to note Unit trust mortgages (like unit-linked endowment mortgages) are more risky than a normal endowment mortgage or a repayment mortgage because the price of your units in the unit trust can fall as well as rise. There might not be enough to pay off the mortgage at the end of the mortgage term if unit prices slump. But, unlike endowment mortgages, unit trust mortgages are very flexible. There are no penalties for cashing in early and nothing to stop you withdrawing your money to pay off the mortgage early. Also, less of your money goes in charges and tax with unit trusts than with unit-linked life insurance.

There's no built-in life insurance with a unit trust mortgage, so if you have dependants you'll need to take out separate protection-only life insurance (see p. 104).

Verdict Unit-linked mortgages are only for those who can take the extra risk, and for many people unit trust mortgages will be a better choice than a unit-linked endowment mortgage.

Other types of mortgages

Fixed interest mortgage The interest rate is fixed for a specified period – say, one, three or five years – when you first take out the loan. After that, the rate becomes variable. There's a penalty charge if you want to switch your mortgage within the fixed interest period. These mortgages are a gamble: if interest rates rise during the fixed interest period, you'll be paying less than with an 'ordinary' mortgage. But if interest rates fall, you'll be stuck paying more.

LIBOR-linked mortgages The interest rate is set at a fixed percentage (one per cent, say) above the three-month London Inter-Bank Offered Rate (LIBOR – the rate at which banks lend to each other). Again, this type of mortgage is a gamble: sometimes you'll be paying more than you would with an 'ordinary' mortgage, sometimes less.

Interest-only mortgages You pay interest only and don't repay the loan until the mortgage ends. Some lenders will lend this way without requiring you to take out an endowment policy or pension plan, and there may be no set mortgage term. Most commonly, this type of mortgage is used with older (40-plus or retired) borrowers, and the loan is repaid from the proceeds of the sale of the home when you move or after you've died. Monthly repayments are lower than for an 'ordinary' mortgage.

Low-start mortgages You pay a lower than normal interest rate, or make interest-only payments, for the first three years, say – though schemes vary. You pay a higher than normal interest rate once the low-start period is over. Useful if you expect your earnings to rise, or if you expect to move again within the low-start period – though watch out for early redemption charges (see p. 35).

Executive or high-earner mortgages You may be able to borrow a higher than normal multiple of your salary, and some lenders let you put off paying part of the interest for a time in a similar way to a low-start scheme (see above). Available to high-flyers whose future career looks promising despite only modest earnings at present.

Larger-than-average mortgages Lenders vary in their treatment of large loans. Some charge a lower rate of interest than on smaller loans if you're borrowing, say, more than £60,000. Other lenders charge more for larger loans – so shop around.

'PEP-linked' mortgages Your monthly payments comprise interest only, and you also invest in a Personal Equity Plan (PEP – see p. 132) which is used eventually to pay off the mortgage. PEPs are a tax-efficient form of investment because there's no income or capital gains tax to pay on the proceeds. But this type of mortgage is more risky than traditional repayment and low-cost endowment mortgages.

Borrowing against your home

Bricks and mortar have traditionally been viewed as a sound investment, particularly over the long term. Even short-term gains can be staggering: for example, over the three years to the end of 1988, house prices in the UK rose by an average of 75 per cent, though increases were considerably lower in Scotland, Northern Ireland and some of the northern areas of England. As a result of rising house prices, many people now have a large pool of untapped capital – 'equity' – over and above the amount of their outstanding mortgage.

You may be happy to leave your capital invested in your home, but it could be a useful source of funds for, say, home improvements, income in retirement, a new car, school fees, or virtually anything you care to think of. There are a number of ways in which you can tap into the equity in your home.

WARNING *Schemes that let you borrow against the value of the equity in your home can be very useful, but don't over-extend yourself and always read the small print before you commit yourself. In particular, bear in mind that house prices can fall as well as rise, so you could be left owing more than your home is worth. And with many schemes you're committed to making regular repayments – if you can't keep these up, the lender can force you to sell your home.*

Extending your mortgage

Where from Existing mortgage lender.

How the scheme works Your mortgage lender may be willing to make you a further loan and add the amount to your existing mortgage. You pay off both loans, either as two separate loans or as one loan made up of the two lumped together.

Points to note You may have to pay for a surveyor to re-value your home. The new loan won't qualify for tax relief. With some lenders, you might find that extending your existing mortgage means that the whole amount you're borrowing is taken out of the MIRAS scheme – this means that your monthly payments will be higher and you'll have to claim tax relief separately from your tax office (or, if you're a non-taxpayer, you won't be able to get tax relief).

Verdict A good loan source, whatever the purpose of the loan. Some lenders charge a bit less where the loan is to be used for home improvements.

TIP *Loans for home improvements (usually extensions to your existing mortgage or second mortgages) used to qualify for tax relief. Since 6 April 1988, they no longer qualify. Existing loans taken out before then continue to get tax relief (though these loans count towards the overall £30,000 limit). If you're getting tax relief on a home improvement loan, be wary of replacing it with another loan – you'll lose the relief.*

Secured loans and second mortgages

Where from Some building societies (may only be offered to existing borrowers), banks, finance houses.

How they work A secured loan is any loan which gives the lender a claim on your property – usually your home – if you fail to keep up the repayments. Because the lender, as a last resort, can force you to sell your home so that they can get back their money, interest rates for secured loans should be lower than for comparable unsecured loans. A mortgage is a secured loan. A second mortgage is the same as a secured loan except that the lender is queuing up for repayment behind your existing mortgage lender.

Interest may be charged at a fixed or a variable rate, and the loan will be for a fixed period of time. Some lenders invite you to take out life insurance to repay the loan (in a similar manner to an endowment mortgage) but this isn't worth doing unless you intend to keep the loan for at least ten years.

You don't have to go to your existing mortgage lender for a secured loan or second mortgage. If you do, it will usually be treated quite separately from your existing mortgage.

Points to note You may have to pay for a surveyor to re-value your home, and there may be an arrangement fee of £50 or so. There may be charges if you want to repay the loan early. Some finance houses in particular, tend to charge fairly high rates of interest, so check other sources. Some lenders charge a bit less where the loan is to be used for home improvements.

Verdict Can be a useful source of loans for any purpose, but only worth considering if you can't get an unsecured loan at a reasonable cost or an extension to your existing mortgage.

'Line of credit' schemes

Where from Banks, building societies, insurance companies, finance houses.

How they work You arrange a secured loan but you don't have to take all of it at once. Instead you borrow when you like, what you like up to the agreed 'credit limit'. With some schemes, you even get a cheque book to use when drawing on the credit. You are charged interest just on the amount actually borrowed and you pay off the loan and interest in monthly payments – either of a set amount, or any amount above a specified minimum (such as three per cent of the amount borrowed or £75 if greater). As you repay the loan, your unused credit rises again, so you can borrow more.

Points to note You'll have to pay for a surveyor to value your home and there'll also be legal fees. There might be an arrangement fee – say, one per cent of the credit limit.

Verdict A flexible and convenient way of tapping into the equity in your home. But an unsecured loan would probably be better if you want to borrow small amounts, and an extension to your mortgage would be better for large one-off sums (for example, to pay for home improvements).

Home income plans

Where from Some insurance companies and some building societies.

How they work You take out a mortgage on your home (there must be no outstanding mortgage already) and use it to buy an annuity – a form of investment which provides you with a regular income for life. You can borrow between 60 and 80 per cent of the value of your home, depending on the scheme. The older you are when you take out the plan, the higher the income you'll get. The plan provider deducts interest (after allowing for tax relief) on the mortgage from the income and hands you the rest. Both the interest on the loan and the income (before interest is deducted) are normally fixed (but see p. 57).

The loan is repaid from the proceeds of selling your home after you die or if you move – though the provider might agree to switch the plan to your new home. If they don't and the mortgage is paid off, the income (which is for life) still continues to be paid and is larger because there are no interest deductions. Couples can take out a joint plan which lasts until both have died.

The maximum loan is usually £30,000 – the largest loan on which you can get tax relief. There's a minimum too – say, £15,000. You can usually take between seven and ten per cent of the mortgage as cash, depending on the scheme.

Points to note You'll have to pay valuation fees and legal fees. The lender might pay for their (but not your) legal fees if the plan goes ahead. Your home remains yours (unlike home reversion schemes – see p. 58), so you benefit from any increases in its value and you could use such increases to take out 'top up' loans to provide further income. Most plans are restricted to people who are 70 or older, and couples may need a combined age of, say, 150. The income from the annuity is made up partly of interest – which is taxable – and partly return of your capital – which is not taxable.

Verdict Home income plans are a useful way of boosting retirement income, though they may turn out to be a bad deal if you're in poor health because the income normally stops when you die regardless of how short a period it has been paid for. Some schemes incorporate a capital protection plan that provides for repayment of part of your capital if you die within the first few years of the plan or guarantees that a minimum amount will be paid even if you die.

WARNING
With annuities, you hand over a lump sum and in return get an income. You can't normally get your capital back as a lump sum. The size of the income you get depends on your sex and your age. Women have a greater life

expectancy than men, so they get less income than a man of the same age. *The older you are, the higher the income. Home income plans are a gamble: if you die shortly after taking out the plan, you'll have had very little of the income, but the whole of the loan has still to be repaid. But the plans can work to your advantage, as in the case of twins who were 100 years old in 1987. They'd borrowed £10,000 through a home income plan in 1973. Because of their longevity they've received far more than that in income.*

TIP *Age Concern produces a useful fact sheet (Number 12) giving details of home income plans – send a large SAE to the address below. It also produces a booklet,* Using your home as capital, *price £1.95. Both can be obtained from:*

Age Concern
60 Pitcairn Road, Mitcham, Surrey CR4 3LL

WARNING *Income from a home income plan may reduce the amount of any state benefits that you're getting.*

Variations on the home income plan theme

Variable interest plans These work like the plans already described, except that the rate of interest on the mortgage rises and falls with the general level of interest rates. The income (before interest has been deducted) from the annuity is fixed, so a rise in the interest rate reduces the amount of income you're left with. Most people should avoid these plans.

Plans linked to other investments Some home income plans don't use some or all of the mortgage loan to buy an annuity. Instead, some or all of the money is invested in single-premium insurance bonds (see p. 126). You can't be sure how much money you'll get from the bonds (as this depends on investment returns) and interest on the mortgage doesn't qualify for tax relief. Avoid these plans.

Variable interest lump sum plans With these, the proceeds of the mortgage provide you with a lump sum instead of an annuity. You can use the money to buy an annuity if you like, but you're then stuck with a fixed income and a variable mortgage rate, so you can't be sure how much income you'll be left with. If you don't buy an annuity, interest on the mortgage doesn't qualify for tax relief. These plans are available to younger people – 60 and upwards – than other home income plans but an annuity will provide a relatively small income unless you're at least 65. Most people should avoid these plans.

Rolled-up interest schemes With these, none of the interest on the mortgage is paid until you die. It's 'rolled up' and repaid along with the loan out of the proceeds of the sale of your home. These plans are risky because the interest mounts up quickly and you can find yourself reaching the limit of borrowing allowed by the lender – you'll then have to pay interest (or, at worst, even sell your home). Also, the rolled-up interest doesn't qualify for tax relief – the taxman argues that you can't get relief after you're dead. Many organisations have lobbied the government to change the law to allow tax relief on rolled-up interest but so far without success.

WARNING

Avoid home reversion schemes. These aren't loan plans. With reversion schemes you sell your house (or part of it) in return for either a lump sum or an income for life plus the right to continue living in the house for the rest of your life. You have to be 65 or more and you remain responsible for maintaining your home. With nearly all the schemes, the company – not you – benefits from any increases in the value of your home after you've taken up the scheme. Instead of one of these schemes, choose a home income plan.

Other types of borrowing

There is a huge range of loans and credit available, many of which are aggressively promoted. Don't be dazzled by the first deal that's thrust upon you. If you shop around, you'll find some deals are much better than others, and some should be avoided altogether.

Overdrafts
Where from Banks, some building societies.

How they work You run a deficit on your current account by spending more than you've got – in other words, you go into the red. It can be a convenient way of borrowing. But it can be expensive: if you don't arrange the overdraft in advance you'll often be charged a penal rate of interest, and even if you do arrange it, you may have to pay bank transaction charges or a standing charge (see p. 72). Building societies and a few banks let you have a limited overdraft and charge you interest only – this is a relatively cheap way of borrowing.

Points to note Some of the accounts offered by building societies and banks have built-in overdrafts – up to £100, say – so you don't need to arrange in advance to go overdrawn. If your account doesn't have a built-in overdraft, bear in mind that you could be asked at any time to pay off what you owe. Usually no security is needed for an overdraft.

Verdict Convenient form of short-term borrowing – useful for, say, buying electrical goods, paying for holidays or covering household bills. Building society and some bank overdrafts are relatively cheap, but other bank overdrafts can be expensive once you take charges into account.

Bank ordinary loans
Where from Banks.

How they work You arrange to borrow a set amount which is then paid into your current account. You then use the money as and when you like. You repay regular amounts into a separate loan account. Interest is variable.

You negotiate the loan individually with your bank manager, so terms may differ from customer to customer. You may be able to borrow more than with other types of loan and for as long as ten years.

Points to note These are very much the Cinderellas among bank loans – they tend not to be advertised and you might be encouraged to take out a personal loan instead. Ordinary loans aren't always available and you're unlikely to get one unless you're an existing customer of the bank. You may have to pay an arrangement fee and the bank might require security – against your home, say.

Verdict Good if you can get them. A flexible and often cheap way of borrowing whether for short-, medium- or fairly long-term purposes – for example, to buy an annual season ticket, a new car, or to pay for home improvements.

Personal loans

Where from Banks, building societies, finance houses.

How they work You borrow a set amount for a specified period – anything from, say, one year up to five or seven years – and you are charged a rate of interest which is fixed at the time you take out the loan. You make regular repayments throughout the term of the loan. There's usually an upper limit on the amount you can borrow – for example, £5,000 or £7,500 with a bank, but more with finance houses and building societies. The latter may be unwilling to lend unless you are an existing customer. There will usually be charges if you want to repay the loan early.

Points to note These loans can be secured (see p. 35) or unsecured. Secured loans will be cheaper than unsecured loans from the same source, but you may find a cheaper unsecured loan from another lender – finance house loans in particular can be relatively expensive. Some lenders – but not all – charge a higher rate of interest on smaller loans (less than £1,000, say) than on larger loans.

Verdict Unsecured bank and building society loans are worth considering if you can't get a bank ordinary loan. They are useful for all kinds of purchases – cars, electrical goods, holidays, and so on. But be wary of taking out a personal loan when interest rates generally seem high – you'll be stuck with the fixed interest rate even if other rates fall. Avoid secured loans unless you are sure you can keep up the repayments.

WARNING *Banks may want loan repayments made direct from your current account with them. Watch out for phrases such as* 'if you don't already have a current account with us, we'll be pleased to open one for you' *which means* 'if you want a loan from us, you must have an account with us'.

TIP *Each summer, when many people are preparing to buy a new car with the latest registration letter on the number plate, many banks offer specially good deals on car loans. But check the terms carefully – a special deal from one source may still not be as good as a loan from another source.*

Bridging loans

Where from Banks, building societies.

How they work You borrow to bridge the gap between paying for your new home and getting the money from the sale of your old home. Loans may be 'open-ended' in which case you borrow for an unspecified length of time because you haven't yet exchanged contracts on your old home. More often, the loan will be 'closed' and will cover the fixed period from exchange of contracts to completion of the sale of the old home. Usually bridging loans aren't secured on either property.

Points to note There may be an arrangement fee of, say, one per cent of the amount borrowed or a flat amount such as £150. The rate of interest is variable and may be quite high. Sometimes you can arrange for the interest to be 'rolled up' and paid when you repay the loan itself. You can get tax relief on the interest on a bridging loan up to £30,000 even if you've used your normal £30,000 limit for mortgage interest relief. Tax relief is normally allowed for up to a year – longer in some cases.

Verdict A closed loan is useful if you really can't synchronise completion dates for both purchase and sale, but it may be expensive. In general, you should avoid open-ended loans – be wary of committing yourself to buying the new home if you haven't got a committed buyer for the old one.

Save and borrow accounts

Where from Banks, some finance houses.

How they work You pay a set amount each month into an account and can borrow up to 30 times the monthly payment. You're charged a variable rate of interest on the amount you actually borrow, and some accounts pay you interest when you're in credit. No security is required.

Points to note Interest on overdrawn accounts tends to be high and there may be other charges. Interest when you're in credit is usually lower than you could get on other interest-bearing accounts.

Verdict Convenient, but expensive.

Budget accounts

Where from Banks, some finance houses.

How they work You add up your expected yearly expenditure and put one-twelfth of the total into the account every month. You then use the account to pay your bills. When you're overdrawn, you pay interest at a variable rate and there may be other charges. You don't get any interest when you're in credit.

Points to note Gas and electricity boards and local authorities run their own schemes for spreading bill payments which generally work out cheaper than using a special budget account. Better still is if you can save regularly in an interest-bearing account and use that to pay the bills (see p. 75).

Verdict May help you to budget, but expensive compared with other options.

Credit cards

Where from Various sources: through banks, building societies, motoring organisations, finance houses, and so on.

How they work With traditional cards, such as the original Visa and Access cards, you have a pre-arranged credit limit and can borrow any amounts up to that limit. You borrow by using your card to pay for goods and services, or to withdraw cash from a cash machine or bank branch. You pay interest on the outstanding balance, and you must pay off a minimum amount each month – usually five per cent of what you owe or £5 if greater – though you can choose to pay more. There's a delay between paying for something with your card and its appearing on a statement which gives you a period of interest-free credit, and if you pay off your bill in full each month you can avoid interest altogether, giving you up to eight weeks' interest-free credit. Credit card borrowing does not require any security.

Many new cards are appearing on the market and some work in different ways from the traditional cards. For example, one card works like a save and borrow account (see p. 61), letting you choose your own monthly repayment and then setting your credit limit at 25 times that amount; another does not let you have a lengthy interest-free credit period if you pay in full, but charges a lower than normal interest rate on outstanding balances; yet another makes an annual charge regardless of the amount you use the card, and then charges a lower than normal interest rate on the outstanding balance.

Points to note Cards might not be accepted in all the places that you shop, but they are now very widely accepted both in the UK and abroad.

Around a half of all cardholders pay off their bills in full each month using their cards as a costless form of 'plastic cheque' – this is particularly useful as most retailers won't accept ordinary cheques without a cheque guarantee card, which may limit your spending to as little as £50 in that way. But for the card companies, this practice is expensive and there are rumblings that a flat fee might be introduced on traditional cards (as has already happened with some of the newer cards) to be paid as well as interest on balances.

Using credit cards to get cash can be expensive. For example, with Visa cards, there's a 1.5 per cent handling charge, as well as any interest you incur. With Access cards, there's no handling charge but you start to run up interest from the date you withdraw the cash.

Verdict Convenient and very flexible. Can be relatively cheap – or even free – if you use credit cards carefully. But they are an expensive way of borrowing if you don't regularly pay off what you owe.

TIP *If you use a credit card to buy goods and services which turn out to be faulty, the Consumer Credit Act 1974 makes the credit card company jointly liable with the supplier for putting matters right. This applies to goods costing between £100 and £30,000 – even if you paid less than £100 by credit card (for example, if you used the card to put down a deposit). If your card was first issued before July 1977, you might find that though the card company will compensate you for the faulty goods or services, it might not pay for any consequential damage (such as spoiled flooring due to the new washing machine leaking) – it's worth applying for a newly issued card because cards issued from July 1977 onwards do give you this protection.*

TIP *If you don't expect to pay off your bill regularly, avoid the traditional credit cards. Instead go for one of the newer cards with a lower interest rate on outstanding balances.*

WARNING
If your credit card is lost or stolen, you are liable for up to £50 of any losses before you've reported the loss to the card company; once you've reported the loss, you have no liability. But you should take care of your card – see p. 82 for tips about doing this.

WARNING
Take sensible precautions when using your credit card to pay for goods and services. For example, never sign a blank voucher, always check the details before signing, and if the 'total' hasn't been written in, insert it yourself before signing. Another precaution you could take is to ask for the discarded carbons from the voucher just to make sure that your card details (which show up clearly on the carbons) aren't left in the waste paper basket where they might subsequently fall into wrong hands.

WARNING
Some credit card issuers automatically increase your credit limit without asking you first. If you're worried that the higher limit might tempt you to spend more than you can afford, ask the issuer to restore the lower limit.

Charge cards and gold cards

Where from Specialist card companies such as American Express, Diners Club, banks.

How they work There's no spending limit and you can use the card to pay for goods and services for any amounts. But you must pay off the whole bill each month. There's an annual fee of anything from £20 to £60, and there may be an initial joining fee. Gold cards are 'up-market' charge cards available to people who can show they have high earnings.

Points to note Charge cards aren't strictly classed as credit cards because you have to pay off your bill each month. But cardholders may have access to cheap loans, and gold cardholders can get special overdrafts on favourable terms.

Verdict Expensive – only worthwhile if, say, you do a lot of business travelling.

Shop credit schemes

Where from Many shops.

How they work Shop credit is a way of paying for goods or services in a particular retailer's shops or other outlets. There are several types of scheme:

- shop cards: these are usually like credit cards though the interest rates are usually much higher. Some shop cards work like save and borrow accounts (see p. 61)
- hire purchase, credit sale and conditional sale: with these, the credit offered is tied to the purchase of particular goods. They work rather like a personal loan – generally, the interest rate is fixed and you make regular payments over a specified period until the loan and interest are paid off. With credit sale, the goods are yours from the outset. But with hire purchase and conditional sale, the goods aren't yours until you've finished paying – though the Consumer Credit Act gives you a certain amount of protection if you can't keep up the repayments (see below). Interest rates tend to be high.

Points to note Shop cards limit you to particular stores – that's fine if you usually shop there anyway but you could be missing out on better bargains elsewhere.

Verdict Convenient – the shop will make the arrangements, but can be expensive (particularly shop cards) so check that you can't borrow more cheaply elsewhere.

WARNING *If you fall behind with the payments for something which you've bought on hire purchase, the supplier can, in certain circumstances, take back the goods. But, if you've paid at least one-third of the total amount payable, the supplier would need a court order before they could do this. If you've paid less than a third, the supplier must send you a formal default notice. This gives you at least seven days within which to bring the payments up to date, in which case, you keep the goods and the hire purchase agreement continues as originally intended.*

TIP *If you can't keep up the payments under a hire purchase deal, you can end the agreement. This means that you return the goods to the supplier, and you have no further payments to make. But the money you've paid so far is deemed to have paid for the hire of the goods over the period you had them, so you get nothing back – not a good deal.*

You must have paid at least half of the amount payable before you can end the deal. If you haven't paid that much, the supplier is legally entitled to demand the balance to take your payments up to the half-way mark. Check the terms for ending a hire purchase deal before you commit yourself to it – notice will normally be required, and you may not be able to end the agreement before it's run for 18 months.

Insurance policy loans

Where from Insurance company with whom you already have an investment-type insurance policy (see p. 104).

How they work You borrow money against the surrender value of the policy to be repaid when the policy matures. The interest rate is variable and tends to be relatively low.

Points to note The maximum loan is a percentage of the surrender value so it might not be much (if anything) if you haven't had the policy long. You can't usually use a policy that's already being used for something else – such as an endowment policy to be used to repay your mortgage. You still have to pay the insurance premiums as well as the repayments on the loan.

Verdict Good source of fairly cheap, long-term borrowing.

Credit unions

Where from Run by the members who all have something in common – for example, they live in the same area, go to the same church, or share the same work.

How they work These are savings and loan co-operatives. Regular saving is encouraged but members can save any amount from £1 up to £2,000. The savings form a pool from which any member can borrow. The maximum you can borrow is £2,000 more than the amount you have saved. The maximum interest rate is set by the Credit Union Act 1979 and is currently fairly low (12.68 per cent APR). Similarly, the maximum interest rate paid on savings is also set by law and is 8 per cent a year – though many unions pay less.

Points to note Credit unions are not common in the UK. You might be interested in starting one yourself – you'll need at least six interested people who must be willing to play an active part in running the credit union. For help and information, contact:

Association of British Credit Unions
48 Maddox Street, London W1R 9BB
Tel: 01-408 1699

National Federation of Savings and Cooperative Credit Unions
1st Floor, Jacob's Well, Bradford BD1 5RW
Tel: 0274 753507

Verdict Relatively cheap source of fairly small loans for any purpose. But depends on whether there's a credit union you can join.

Moneylenders

Where from Bona fide ones: mainly through newspaper advertisements.

How they work They specialise in high-risk lending and charge dearly as a result. Loans may be secured or unsecured. Interest rates may be fixed or variable. They may lend to you even if you've been unable to borrow elsewhere. Repayments are often collected door-to-door.

Points to watch At the time of writing, moneylenders who lend sums in excess of £30 have, by law, to be licensed. (And there are proposals that even those lending smaller sums should, in future, need a licence.) But some moneylenders make loans above the £30 limit without being licensed – they trade illegally. Such lenders are sometimes known as 'loan sharks' and usually charge high interest rates which, in some cases, work out at APRs (see p. 37) of several thousand per cent. But even licensed moneylenders can charge fairly steep rates of interest and are generally an expensive source of credit. If you suspect that a moneylender is unlicensed, report them to your local Trading Standards Department or the police. If you feel hopelessly in debt to a moneylender, you should seek help from a debt counsellor (see p. 40).

Verdict Avoid.

WARNING *Moneylenders, both licensed and unlicensed, have been known to ask for (and, in some cases, seize) child allowance, pension or social security benefit books as* *security for loans. This practice is illegal. Never part with these documents in such circumstances. Inform the police or the Trading Standards Department if a moneylender suggests such a course of action.*

Trading checks

Where from Trading check companies.

How they work A trading check is a document with a value normally between £1 and £30 which can be exchanged for goods in specified shops. Each purchase is deducted from the value of the check. 'Vouchers' are similar to trading checks but may be valued up to £500 and can usually be used only to make specific, more expensive purchases in specified shops.

Trading checks are delivered to the borrower by an agent who then calls each week to collect repayments. These are fixed at the outset and are usually spread over a period of 20 or 21 weeks. With vouchers, the repayments are usually over a period of two or three years. APRs are quite high – 60 per cent up to several hundred per cent.

Points to note The shops you can use checks and vouchers in may not be the cheapest for the goods you're buying. Check traders issuing checks only up to £30 don't have to be licensed.

Verdict Avoid.

4

Day-to-day finances

Bankers are just like anybody else, except richer.
Ogden Nash

Current accounts are central to managing your money on a day-to-day basis. They were once the exclusive preserve of the banks. But since the Building Societies Act 1986 opened the way for building societies to offer many new services, the distinction between banks and building societies has become increasingly blurred, especially in the area of personal banking. What you might expect from a current account is also changing: standard services include not just the usual cheque book, cash card, standing order and direct debit. There are new electronic services as well, including home banking and new ways to pay in shops.

What's on offer is widely promoted. Less clear sometimes are the potential costs involved in using some of these services, and the rights and obligations of you, the customer, and of the bank or building society. This chapter looks at the main problem areas and tells you how to avoid or mitigate their effects.

What current accounts offer

The services associated with current accounts are:
- cheque book: this is the most commonly used alternative to paying for items by cash. Some of the building society accounts and a few bank accounts don't include a cheque book – a serious drawback for most people
- cheque guarantee card: this ensures that your bank will pay out on a cheque up to a given limit. In most cases, the limit is £50, though it's £100 with some accounts, and some banks will issue to particular customers cards with a limit up to £250. The card

guarantees that the person you're paying will get their money (up to the limit) regardless of whether you have enough money in your account, and you'll have to produce the card in most places where you pay for goods or services with a cheque

- cash card: you can use this in 'hole in the wall' machines (Automated Teller Machines – ATMs) to withdraw cash from your account. Many ATMs also let you check your balance, order statements or cheque books and sometimes give you mini-statements and let you pay bills too
- standing orders and direct debits: these are methods of making regular payments, such as paying insurance premiums, or rent or mortgage payments, or transferring part of your salary to a savings account
- debit card: a plastic card which you use instead of cheques and which automatically debits your current account when you use it to buy goods and services
- home banking: the big banks (and a few building societies) now offer a service which lets you conduct much of your banking from home using either just your phone, or your phone in conjunction with a home computer or Prestel receiver and TV

WARNING *Banking from home is clearly convenient, but unless you already have the necessary equipment it can be expensive. The cheapest systems use your phone plus a tone pad – but you won't need the tone pad if your phone is one which can use tone dialling. For the systems which use Prestel, you'll need Prestel equipment or a computer. Check what the running costs will be as well, before committing yourself to this type of banking.*

- overdraft facility: you may be allowed to have access to more money than is in your account – up to a limit
- interest paid on your balance while you're in credit: this is not a feature of traditional bank accounts but is standard with building society accounts and newer accounts from big banks

WARNING *Some 'high interest' accounts restrict your banking in various ways – for example, there may be no cheque card or cash card, or you may need to keep a minimum balance of £500, say, or withdrawals may have to be a minimum size such as £100 or £200. For most people, these restrictions mean that such accounts are not suitable for their day-to-day finances.*

Current account charges

Charges when you're in credit

All the major banks, and the building societies which offer current accounts, offer 'free banking' as long as your account is in credit – this means that you pay no charges for the standard services such as payments by cheque, standing order or direct debit, or cash card withdrawals. But even if you're in the black, banks may charge you for a variety of other fairly humdrum services – see the Table below. Building societies offer fewer extra services and, where they do, they're less likely to charge.

Extra Current Account Charges

Service	Example of charges
Duplicate statement	From nothing to several ££s for each page
Stopping a cheque	From nothing to several ££s You might also be charged if someone stops a cheque for you
Special presentation of a cheque (to get it cleared in less time than usual)	From nothing to several ££s
Bounced cheque – you may be charged if a cheque you pay into your account bounces	From 50p to several ££s
Banker's draft (used mainly for paying large sums when a cheque won't be accepted)	From nothing to £10 or more
Cashing a cheque at another branch (eg for cheques over the guarantee card limit, or for less than this but without presenting your cheque guarantee card or cash card)	From nothing to about £3
Arranging 'open credit' so that you can draw cash regularly at a different branch from yours without using a cheque card	From nothing to about £10
Getting a bank reference if you want to check the financial standing of someone you do business with. (You don't pay if the bank is asked for a reference about you)	From nothing to several ££s

TIP *Banks don't always inform you about charges for extra services when you open the account, and some charges are at the manager's discretion, so make a point of asking for details.*

Charges when you're overdrawn

Putting your current account into overdraft means you pay extra. You'll have to pay interest on the amount you borrow (which will usually be at a higher rate than normal if you haven't arranged in advance to have an overdraft). But the amount of interest won't usually be very great if you slip into the red only occasionally. The real problem with most bank accounts – but not with building society accounts – is charges:

- transaction charges: with most traditional bank accounts, if you're overdrawn, you have to pay around 20p to 40p in charges every time money is withdrawn from your account (whether by cheque, cash card, standing order or direct debit) and in some cases you have to pay when money is credited to your account, too; the charges are made throughout the 'charging period' even if you're overdrawn for just one day in the period. Charging periods vary – with one bank it's one month, but with most it's three months. On top of transaction charges, there might be a flat charge of, say, £3 per charging period. Charges will generally be waived if your average balance for the charging period is above a certain level – £500, perhaps

- flat fee: many newer bank accounts charge you a flat fee when you're overdrawn instead of making transaction charges. The fee could be anything from a few ££s up to £30 or so a month

- arrangement or administration fee: if you do things properly and arrange your overdraft beforehand, you're likely to face an arrangement fee of around £10 to £25. If you don't arrange the overdraft, your bank might let you overdraw up to a limit but there could be an administration fee for doing this

- other charges: if your cheques are bounced you may be charged up to £15 or so for each cheque. You may also have to pay up to £10 apiece for letters from the bank warning you that you're overdrawn.

TIP *Always ask about related costs – such as transaction charges and arrangement fees – before you arrange an overdraft. You may find that it's easier and cheaper to use your credit card for occasional overspending.*

CASE HISTORY

Through an oversight Mrs E went overdrawn on her current account for two days. When her next statement arrived she found that she had been charged well over £30 – nearly twice the amount of the overdraft. The charges were so high because the bank, like many others, operated on a three-month charging period: for every debit transaction – cheques, cash from dispensers, standing orders, direct debits – she was charged 28p, plus a maintenance charge of several pounds. It could have been worse – she didn't get a letter warning about the unauthorised overdraft and none of her cheques bounced (some banks charge £5 or £10 for these). There were no charges for credit transactions, either.

Moral: consider switching to an account, such as those increasingly available from building societies and some banks, which charge interest only for the time you're overdrawn.

WARNING *Some accounts automatically fix an overdraft limit when you open the account which means that there's no arrangement fee when you want to overdraw, and there may be no other charges as long as you stay within the limit. But you should still get permission before going overdrawn, otherwise you'll probably incur an administration charge and other charges. Some charges are at the manager's discretion, so it's extremely difficult to tell in advance how much going overdrawn will cost you overall.*

TIP *If you accidentally go overdrawn and you're not often in the red, it's worth asking the manager to waive the charges. This may happen, especially if you are looked on as a particularly valued customer.*

With some newer bank accounts, there's a built-in interest-free and charge-free overdraft. The amount you can borrow is limited – for example, a maximum of £250, and instead of interest and charges, you pay a flat fee of around £10 a month both when overdrawn and when in credit. You know exactly where you stand with these accounts, but for most people they work out more expensive than accounts charging only when overdrawn.

TIP *Building society accounts usually work out cheapest if you tend to go overdrawn, because there's normally only interest to pay but no transaction or other charges. At least two banks also offer overdrafts on this basis.*

Keeping the costs down

Even the most careful customer can slip up from time to time, but there are steps you can take to reduce the likelihood of going overdrawn, and to keep the costs down if you do go briefly into the red:

- get your salary paid directly into your account. You'll be able to get at your money more quickly than if you have to pay it in by cheque
- try to fix standing order and direct debit dates soon after your salary has been paid in. It's more likely that funds will be available then and less likely that you'll overlook regular bills when working out how much you've got left to spend
- make sure money paid into your account has 'cleared' before you try to draw it out. It normally takes *at least* three working days for a cheque to clear – that is, for the bank or building society to be reassured that the cheque isn't going to bounce. With building society accounts especially, it can take seven working days or more. (Watch out for weekends and bank holidays – these will delay clearance.) If you try to withdraw uncleared money, you might find that your request is refused, or that you incur administration and other charges even though your account appears, on the face of it, not to have been overdrawn. Unfortunately most bank statements don't differentiate between cleared and uncleared amounts in your account – building society statements usually do. If you're not sure whether your money has cleared, ask your branch to check for you
- if you need an overdraft, arrange it with your branch manager first. If you accidentally dip into the red, contact your branch manager as soon as possible. If you'll have to pay transaction charges, use the account as little as possible – use your credit card whenever possible instead of writing cheques for each purchase, then pay off the credit card each month with just one cheque.

Choosing a current account

Before you open a current account, decide what your needs are and take time to look for the account with features best suited to your needs.

Why give away interest?

Even if you don't have much money left in your account by the end of the month, your average balance could still be high enough to earn you, say, £20 or £30 interest a year – perhaps more. It's not much but why give it to your bank when both banks and building societies offer interest-earning current accounts?

TIP *Unless you're particularly looking for a 'high interest' account (see p. 70), don't bother shopping around for the current account with the best interest rate – the difference between the best and worst is likely to be less than £10 a year. Other features – particularly charges – are likely to be more important when selecting an account.*

Paying bills

There are several ways you can arrange for paying bills. A standing order is useful for regular bills of a fixed amount – such as local authority rates instalments. But for bills which vary in size – such as mortgage repayments – direct debits can be more convenient because the person you're paying debits your account for whatever's due without your having to alter the amount.

Some accounts let you pay bills using a cash machine. Initially, you'll have to give your branch details of who is to be paid and their account number. When you want to pay, you call up the 'screen' for that bill and key in the amount to be paid. You'll usually need to allow up to six working days for the payment to go through.

Home banking lets you pay bills from your armchair – again, initially you'll need to give your bank details of who's to be paid and their account number.

TIP *If you have a bad memory, standing orders and direct debits may suit you better than arrangements where you have to remember to pay.*

Keeping track

You'll usually get a statement of your account automatically several times a year. You can get more frequent statements if you ask – normally there's no charge as long as your account is in credit. If you want to keep a closer check on your account, building societies tend to have the edge. Their computer systems mean that your statements are more likely to be up to date and they'll also show you what proportion of your balance is made up of uncleared cheques. Some societies offer free 'mini-statements' showing your last ten or so transactions – you can get these at any branch or through cash machines, in some cases. Banks with new computer systems can usually offer these facilities too.

If you're happy just to keep track of your balance, you should go for a bank or building society with a large cash machine network. Traditionally, the banks have done well on this score, but in autumn 1989 the Link and Matrix networks are due to merge, which will make one of the largest networks.

Getting at your cash

If you usually need to get at your money soon after paying cheques in, you might be frustrated by most building society accounts – commonly it takes seven working days for cheques paid in to clear. This delay happens because most building societies don't belong to the 'clearing system' and have themselves to pay into a bank which is a member of the system. If your account is with a bank (all the big banks and several others) or one of the few building societies (Abbey National and Nationwide Anglia) which belong to the clearing system, cheques that you pay in should normally take only about three days to clear though you should check what's usual for the particular bank or society before you decide to open an account.

It's quite feasible to run a current account without ever visiting a branch, but once in a while you may want to do business in person – for example, if you're seeking a loan, or trying to sort out a problem with your account – so it's usually sensible to open an account at a branch that's conveniently close to home or where you work. If you move around a lot, a large branch network may be important to you. The major banks have far more branches than even the largest building societies – for example, National Westminster Bank has over 3,000 branches compared with around 900 for Nationwide Anglia Building

Society. The biggest network of all is that of Girobank which operates through 20,000 post office branches.

If you can't usually get to a branch during opening hours, you may be more concerned about a large cash machine network. Banks and building societies have been joining forces to increase these networks, so you can use most cash cards in a number of different banks' and societies' machines.

If there's no branch or cash machine to hand, you can cash a bank cheque at any other bank, but you may have to pay up to £3 or so for this service. You'll have to pay the cost of a phone call too, if the cheque is for more than the amount covered by your cheque guarantee card. You can't cash a building society cheque at a bank unless there's a special arrangement.

Your rights and responsibilities

The basic contract

You might not sign a formal agreement when you open a current account, but nonetheless a contract between you and the bank or building society exists, and there are a whole host of 'implied terms' that you might not be aware of until things go wrong. Your relationship with a bank is also affected by various Acts of Parliament as well as a vast body of case law which has grown up over the years. Building societies' banking services are much more recent – they are covered by the Building Societies Act 1986. Most of this section is concerned with the rights and obligations relating to bank accounts but many of the points discussed are relevant to building society accounts as well.

A bank's main duties to you are to receive your money and to hold it for you until you give the bank instructions to pay it back to you or to someone else. The bank should use reasonable care and skill in carrying out these duties. On your part, you should take reasonable care in making your instructions so that you neither mislead the bank nor encourage fraud.

Many banks and building societies produce leaflets giving details of the terms and conditions of their current accounts. These are sometimes weighted in favour of the bank and make assumptions about your agreeing to various terms, such as disclosure of your affairs (see p. 87). And the terms and conditions are sometimes changed overnight. A recent review of the services provided by banks (by the Review Committee on Banking Services Law – known as the 'Jack Committee') has suggested that banks should make a much better effort to communicate to you their terms and conditions, and that you should be given a fair and balanced view of the rights and obligations of both you, as customer, and the bank. The Committee also recommended that banks should give you notice of any change to the terms and conditions applying to an account.

Cheques

One of the key features of a current account is the cheque. In spite of an increasing tide of plastic money, cheques are made out by the million every day and still account for over half of all non-cash transactions.

Writing cheques A bank must pay out on a cheque which has been properly drawn by the account holder, as long as the account is in credit, or there's an agreed overdraft limit. You should take care when writing a cheque to prevent the possibility of someone else altering it. If you write a sloppy cheque that allows room for alteration, you – not the bank – could be liable for the money lost. If the words and figures on a cheque disagree, it is the words which legally take precedence. In practice, your bank might decide to pay the lower amount, or to return the cheque to you for clarification. Points to watch out for when writing a cheque are:

- never use pencil or a pen that can be rubbed out
- always write the words close together to limit the scope for alteration – for example 'eight' can fairly easily be amended to 'eighty', and if you leave a gap in the box for the figures too, you could be in for trouble
- don't leave gaps in the figure box or after the words – instead draw a line along the empty space
- never sign a cheque before it has been fully completed and is about to be used.

Crossed cheques A source of great confusion is the use and meaning of a crossing on a cheque. Crossed cheques (which are now standard for most personal cheque books) must be paid into bank accounts – they can't just be exchanged for cash. Cheques are always transferable – you can pass on a cheque made out to you to someone else for them to pay into their account as long as you endorse the cheque with your signature. But you can write 'Not negotiable' on a cheque which means that whoever it's passed on to can't have a better right to payment than the person who passed it on had – so if it's a stolen or forged cheque, there can be no claim on the person who wrote the cheque and it should be worthless. It's fairly common practice to write 'Account payee' or 'Account payee only' across the crossing on a cheque – the intention is to make sure that the cheque is paid only into the account of the person to whom the cheque's made out. But in fact these phrases have no statutory significance at all and are not as effective as you might think.

Out-of-date cheques A cheque once written must be presented at the bank on which it's drawn within a reasonable time – most banks allow six months. After that, the cheque is no longer valid.

Forged cheques When you open an account, you're asked to provide a specimen signature. This enables your bank to check whether cheques bearing your signature seem really to have been signed by you rather than someone trying to forge your signature. The bank must not pay out on a cheque where the signature is not yours, and it would normally be wholly liable for any loss if it paid out against a forged cheque – no matter how skilful the forgery. But you could be liable if you suspected that the forgery had taken place or could have done (for example, if you'd lost your cheque book) and failed to alert your bank.

Signatures change, and though banks don't normally ask you for a repeat specimen of your signature, it would be a good idea to provide a new one if you're aware that yours has changed.

WARNING *If a cheque is stolen, it's easy for a thief to open an account at a building society or bank in the name of the person to whom the cheque is written and then withdraw the money a few days later. This is possible because, while many building societies ask for a specimen signature, they don't normally check the identity of the person opening the account, and though banks will usually ask for some proof of identity (for example, a passport or driving licence), this may have been stolen along with the cheque book. At one time, banks always took up references on new customers but most no longer do so. The Jack Committee (see opposite) has recommended that checks should be made on new customers to reduce the likelihood of this type of crime.*

Bounced cheques If a cheque is backed by a guarantee card, it must be honoured by your bank even if there isn't enough money in your account. But without the back-up of a guarantee card, the bank is not legally obliged to pay out a penny more than the amount in your account. In practice, the bank will often pay out if only a small amount is involved, or if you're a trusted customer, or if they know money is shortly to be paid in. If there's enough money in the account to meet some cheques but not others the bank manager is entitled to decide which should be paid and which bounced – he'll try to pay those which seem most important, and ideally he'll get in contact with you before deciding.

WARNING *Never assume that your bank will let you run up an overdraft if you haven't arranged it first – it might not. And bear in mind that deliberately to write cheques backed by a guarantee card when you know there's not enough money in your account could be construed as theft in England or fraud under Scottish law.*

Note In Scotland, special rules apply if your bank decides not to pay out on cheques written against an account with insufficient money in it. The real problem arises where several cheques arrive at once – the bank is obliged to pay out on none of them and to transfer any money in your account to a special 'suspense account'. This happens even if you have enough money to meet at least some of the cheques. The money can be released from the suspense account only if you pay into your current account enough money to meet all the cheques, or the holders of the cheques give up their claims on you, or five years have passed, or there's a legal ruling about the account. So dipping into the red in Scotland can seriously disrupt your finances.

Stopping cheques If you've written a cheque but then decide you don't want to pay after all – for example, if you've bought goods that turn out to be faulty or don't turn up – you can ask your bank to stop the cheque. You'll need to act quickly – an initial phone call to the bank should put the cheque on hold. You should then put your instructions in writing and send them to the bank. There's usually a charge for stopping a cheque.

WARNING *You can't stop a cheque backed by a cheque guarantee card.*

Standing orders and direct debits

The technical banking term for standing orders and direct debits is 'pre-authorised payments'. In other words, they are arrangements agreed in advance and in writing for the payment of given amounts at given times. Your bank or building society will continue the pattern of payments until you instruct in writing that they be altered or discontinued – you may be required to give a period of notice. Standing orders are the older of the two systems but have to some extent been superseded by direct debits which now account for one in eleven of all non-cash transactions.

Standing orders This mechanism is most useful where you need to pay equal amounts at regular intervals – for example £50 on the first day of every month. You can use it to pay anyone who has a banking account. You instruct your bank to make payments from your account but if, say, the amount to be paid changes you'll have to tell your bank or building society to amend the arrangement. It's not a very convenient system if the amount to be paid changes often.

Direct debits This is a more flexible system. Direct debits can be set up to pay either fixed or variable amounts at regular intervals. You instruct your bank to allow payments to be made from your account at the request of the organisation that you are paying and in accordance with the direct debit agreement. Usually the organisation provides a prepared form for you to complete and give to your bank.

Letting an organisation take money from your account in this way might, on the face of it, seem a bit risky. But careful checks are made on organisations wishing to operate direct debit schemes, and they must abide by stringent rules. In particular, the amount payable under a variable direct debit can be altered only after you've been given 14 days' notice of the change. If you're not happy with the new amount, you can instruct your bank to cancel the arrangement.

TIP *Standing orders and direct debits are useful ways to help you plan for regular bills and ensure that they are paid on time. But occasionally, check on your account statements that payments are being made correctly – a mistake over paying insurance premiums, say, could leave you without cover. And note that, if a bank can't pay your standing order on the due date because there's not enough money in your account, it's not under any duty to make the payment once more money is paid in – it's up to you to make sure that the payments are brought up to date.*

TIP *A supplier of goods or services can legally insist that payment should normally be by some particular method. But if you're not happy making payments by direct debit, try asking the organisation if they'll accept payment by another method. Many will agree. If they don't and you feel strongly about it, you'll have to take your custom elsewhere.*

Cash cards

Over 35 million cash cards have been issued in the UK and there are a further 25 million credit cards most of which can also be used to get cash. With over 12,500 cash machines available, cash cards have generally made life easier. But they have also brought problems. The Jack Committee (see p. 78) reported that ATM disputes (in other words, disputes concerning the use of Automated Teller Machines or cash machines) are running at a rate of one every hour in the UK. ATM disputes are the largest area of work for the Banking Ombudsman (see p. 163) and the second largest for the Building Societies Ombudsman (see p. 164) after mortgage related disputes.

Lost or stolen cards You are particularly vulnerable in the case of cash cards because they fall outside the legislation that covers other payment methods such as credit cards or cheques. So the banks and building societies have largely written their own rules and have put an enormous obligation on you as cardholder. Usually, you are liable for *all transactions authorised by the cash card*. This means that you are liable for all amounts paid out through use of the card whether or not you were the one using it. The liability ceases once you notify the bank or building society that your card is lost or stolen or likely to be misused for some other reason. Some card issuers – but not all – limit your liability before notification to a maximum sum, such as £50. The Jack Committee has recommended that your liability should be limited in this way with all cash cards (see p. 87).

WARNING *If your cash card is lost or stolen, notify your bank or building society at once. But note that phoning, or even going to your branch in person, is not enough by itself. You must confirm the notification in writing (by fax if you like) and normally within a given time limit – for example, seven days. There are several card notification companies which for a fee keep a record of all your card numbers and will ring all your card issuers if your cards are lost or stolen. This is a potentially very useful service since you need to keep only the emergency phone number of the notification company rather than those* *of all your card issuers. But the legal position regarding these notification services is not entirely clear: will all your card issuers accept notification from the company, do you still need to confirm the notification yourself and how rapidly, who's liable if the notification company makes a mistake? Check these points with the bank or building society which issued each of your cards before you rely on a notification service.*

Security A weakness of cash cards – and most other plastic cards at present – is the way in which transactions are authorised. In most cases, this is done by keying a number – your Personal Identification Number or PIN – into a machine. The trouble is that your PIN is not truly personal in the way that a written signature is – anyone getting hold of your card and PIN can use your account. Therefore, efficient security is vital to this type of system: you must guard your card and your PIN, but the bank or building society should also make sure that their procedures (for example, for issuing new cards and PINs) and equipment are secure.

No machine or computer is perfect. But though most banks or building societies admit to an occasional mechanical error resulting in a cash machine paying out less than it should, they are reluctant to admit that unauthorised withdrawals are possible. So if you are the victim of a 'phantom withdrawal' – a cash machine withdrawal which you didn't

CASE HISTORY

When Mrs V disputed six withdrawals from the automatic cash machine totalling several hundred pounds, her bank insisted that it was not their fault. Eventually she went to the police who assumed that one of her teenage sons had used her card, but Mrs V never told anyone of her PIN. Mrs V was unlucky in that she never recovered the money, nor did she receive an apology or satisfactory explanation.

However, bank cash machines can *make mistakes – there have been cases of banks allocating an incorrect number, for instance. But if the bank is adamant that there has not been a mistake, the customer is in a very weak position. Even customers with a cast-iron alibi for the time of the disputed withdrawal may find the bank suspecting that the card was 'borrowed'.*

make appearing on your statement – the suspicion will be that you haven't adequately safeguarded your card and PIN. Yet the Jack Committee was advised of various cash card crimes: it is apparently fairly easy for a thief to overlook a customer keying in his or her PIN and subsequently steal the card. One case involved using an electronic device to 'tap' information recorded on the cash card's magnetic strip as it was used in the machine, and stolen cards can be wiped clean and loaded with a new PIN belonging to another cardholder.

The Jack Committee has recommended that banks improve cash machine security in a number of ways – for example, they should improve screening around machines to prevent customers being over-looked, and they should use computer systems to spot and monitor suspicious cash machine withdrawal patterns.

Self-defence Take steps to minimise the likelihood of your cash card (or other plastic card, such as a credit card) being misused:
• when you're issued with a PIN memorise it and then destroy the written record. If you forget your PIN, you can always request a new one

- if the envelope containing your notification of a new PIN is torn or looks as if it might have been tampered with, phone the card issuer and ask for the PIN to be cancelled and replaced by a new one
- don't disclose your PIN to anyone – however trustworthy they seem. Even members of your own family can fall under suspicion – for their own protection, it's better that they don't know your PIN
- look after your card. Check regularly that it's still in your possession, and notify the card issuer immediately if you can't find it
- when using a cash machine, make it difficult for anyone to pick up your PIN by shielding the keyboard with your hand or body and punching in your number quickly
- if a printed record of the transaction is available, take it, check that it's correct, and keep it. The Jack Committee has recommended that all cash machines should give you the option of a printed receipt
- keep your own record of dates and times and amounts of withdrawals – this is especially important if the machine hasn't provided a receipt
- if the machine gives you less cash than you asked for, try to get someone in the queue to witness the fact, and get their name and address to give to the bank or building society
- check your statements to make sure that cash machine withdrawals are shown correctly
- if your statement shows a withdrawal that you're certain you didn't make, tell your bank or building society as soon as possible. Provide them with copies of all the relevant printed receipts and a copy of your written record. Give them details of your whereabouts on the day of the disputed withdrawal. Ask the manager (not any other member of staff) to investigate. To protect yourself from any more 'phantom withdrawals' you could ask the bank or building society to retain your card until the matter is resolved. Alternatively, ask the bank to cancel that card or PIN and issue you with a new one.

Debit cards and EFT-POS

Debit cards are, in essence, a plastic cheque which you use to withdraw or transfer money from your account. Technically, a cash card is a debit card – though it's rarely described as such. The use of debit cards to pay for goods and services, rather than just as a means of getting cash, is relatively new. Their use is likely to increase with the growth of EFT-POS.

EFT-POS This stands for Electronic Funds Transfer at Point of Sale. It means paying for goods and services using computer terminals in the shop, petrol station or wherever. There are already a number of EFT-POS schemes. Payments are made using credit cards and/or debit cards. Your card is 'swiped' through a point-of-sale terminal and you are asked to authorise the payment by either signing a form produced by the terminal or by punching your PIN into a keypad. If the system is 'on-line' it can 'talk' directly to your bank's or building society's computer to check that you have sufficient money in your account or that you're within your credit limit, and immediately debit you for the amount paid. If the system is 'off line' it will store details of the transaction which will be passed to your bank or building society later through a clearing system. With an off-line system, the point-of-sale terminal may itself have a limit on the size of transaction that it will accept. With an on-line system, your PIN may be checked for authenticity against a distant database, or with either system the PIN may be checked against data recorded on the card itself.

As long as EFT-POS uses PINs for authorising transactions, it suffers from the same susceptibility to fraud as the cash card system (see p. 82 to 84). But new types of card and new methods of authorisation are being developed. 'Smart' or 'memory' cards contain their own microprocessor which can be loaded with data, such as a spending limit, and programmed to record transaction details and reduce the available balance. It's alleged that smart cards are virtually impossible to forge without the manufacturer's equipment.

Two new authentication systems are under investigation which if used in conjunction with smart cards would greatly increase the security of card payment systems. With electronic signature recognition you'd use your written signature as you do now with cheques and so on. The electronic checking is claimed to be more reliable than visual checking by a shop assistant or bank clerk. Biometric identification techniques are perhaps more controversial – they would rely on checking some exclusively personal characteristic, such as your fingerprint, palmprint, voice, retina, or even analysing your veins or saliva. Out of these, fingerprint recognition is thought to be the most likely to be acceptable.

Debit cards Many current EFT-POS schemes are pilot projects so you might not have the option to try them out just yet. But debit cards are a possibility for anyone and are issued by most of the big banks. Before applying for a debit card, bear in mind these points:

- using a debit card rather than a cheque usually means that your account is debited much sooner than the three days or more that it normally takes for a transaction to clear
- using a debit card rather than a credit card means that you lose an interest-free period of credit
- the legal position regarding debit cards is unclear so it's important to check the terms and conditions – in particular, whether your liability is limited if the card is lost or stolen. The Jack Committee has proposed that debit cards – including cash cards – should be brought into line with credit cards. With these, the Consumer Credit Act 1974 limits the cardholder's liability to a maximum of £50 up to the time the loss or theft is notified, with no liability after that – though a cardholder could be liable for all losses if they'd been negligent.

Keeping things confidential

Banks and building societies have a well-established duty to keep details of their customers' accounts confidential. Employees have to sign declarations of confidentiality and are not allowed to discuss customers' business outside the bank – or even inside if there's a possibility of being overheard.

Anyone – including you – should get short shrift if they ring up your branch asking for details of your account over the phone. If you go into a branch and ask for details of your balance, the amount should be written down and handed to you, not spoken aloud.

If you're not satisfied with the security at your branch, discuss it with the manager. If you know someone at the branch personally and feel uncomfortable about them having access to your account details, your only recourse is to switch to another branch.

In some instances, banks are obliged to supply information about their customers' accounts:

- where required to by law – for example, providing the Inland Revenue with a list of customers who receive more than a given amount of interest (this applies also to building societies), or communicating a suspicion that a customer's funds are derived from drug trafficking

- where it's a public duty. In practice, most instances of this nature are now covered by specific laws
- where it's in the interests of the bank. This is a very vague area. It seems reasonable enough that the bank should use such information to prevent itself from, say, advancing a loan to a customer who was a bad risk. But it's not reasonable that information about a customer's personal details or banking habits should fuel, say, the direct marketing of other services offered by the bank, such as insurance sales or investment advice. The Jack Committee has recommended that this duty to disclose be strictly limited
- where you have given your consent – even if it's only implied. For example, you'll usually be deemed to have given your implied consent to the bank responding to requests for a bank reference. The Jack Committee has recommended that banks should seek your specific consent before they divulge particular information
- where your relationship with the bank has broken down. For example, banks have recently begun to pass information about customers' bad debts to credit reference agencies (see p. 32). It's argued that this can be done without getting consent because, by going into debt, the customer has broken the contract with the bank and caused the relationship to break down.

TIP *Under the Data Protection Act 1984 you have a right to a written record of any data about yourself which is held on computer record. Even if you can't prevent the bank disclosing information in some circumstances, you may at least be able to obtain a copy of the information passed on.*

Complaints

Mistakes can happen but the damage can often be minimised if you spot them quickly and take steps to get matters put right.

Always check your bank statements. Though there's no legal obligation to do this (as there is in some countries) it may alert you to any error.

If you find a mistake, contact your branch as soon as possible. If you make a personal visit, take with you any relevant papers, such as records of cash withdrawals, copies of direct debit forms, and so on. If the problem is complex, it might be helpful to take along a brief written summary of the facts. If the counter staff can't sort out the problem, insist on seeing the manager. If you can't visit your branch, put your complaint in writing, enclose copies (never originals) of the relevant papers and send it all to the branch manager.

If your branch can't resolve the matter to your satisfaction, write to the head office – if you don't know whom to contact there, address your letter to the Customer Relations Manager or phone the head office first to find out who deals with such problems. Once again, enclose copies of the relevant documents with your letter.

If you have no joy with head office either, then you may be able to take your case to the relevant Ombudsman. The Banking Ombudsman scheme is a voluntary one. Not all banks belong to it, though all the major ones do. If your bank is not a member, the Ombudsman won't be able to look into your case, and your only remaining course of action might be to take the matter to court. The Building Society Ombudsman is a statutory scheme to which all building societies must belong. Details of both these schemes are given in Chapter 8.

If you're not happy with the Ombudsman's decision, you can go to court – but this could be a very costly and lengthy procedure.

TIP *If you become so fed up with your bank or building society that you decide to move your account, don't act in haste. Open a new account first. Once you've got a cheque book, guarantee card and cash card, and have set up your standing orders and direct debits, you can safely close the old account with the minimum of inconvenience.*

5

Buying insurance

Simply by not owning three medium-sized castles in Tuscany I have saved sufficient money in the last forty years in Insurance Premiums alone *to buy a medium-sized castle in Tuscany.* Punch, 1974

Nobody likes to dwell on disasters, but accidents, fires, thefts, illnesses and death don't only just happen to other people. Insurance can't stop these things happening to you, but it can prevent financial hardship as a result. That doesn't mean that you must take out every kind of insurance available. The things which you are most likely to want to insure are:

- your home. If you own or are buying your own home, you need house buildings insurance
- your belongings. You need house contents insurance for things like your clothes, books, cameras, furniture and carpets
- your means of transport. By law, you must have at least some insurance if you run a car (or various other vehicles, such as a motorbike)
- your life. If anyone – children, wife, elderly parents and so on – is dependent on you and would suffer financially if you were to die, you need life insurance
- your health. If you'd be hard up if you had to stop work for a long time due to illness or disability, you should consider permanent health insurance – particularly if you're self-employed
- your holiday. If you're going on holiday – particularly abroad – you'll usually need holiday insurance.

What insurance does

The aim of insurance is to compensate you following a loss so that you're as well off – but no better off – than you were before the loss occurred. The exception is life insurance (often called *as*surance); since a value can't be put on human life, it's up to you to decide how much cover you want.

An insurance policy is a contract and your rights as policyholder depend entirely on what is written in it and on any endorsements which may be tacked on. You can choose different companies and policies, but you have very little chance of influencing the terms of a particular contract. For the most part, you get the cover that the insurer is willing to offer. Insurance contracts are not covered by the Unfair Contract Terms Act 1977, so they can still rely on exclusion clauses.

In several of his annual reports, the Insurance Ombudsman (see p. 158) has pointed to 'the apparent gap between promise and achievement' with many types of insurance. That gap has resulted in so much dissatisfaction and disappointment that the Ombudsman has even suggested that all glossy brochures for house insurance should carry a health warning drawing attention to the facts that:

- no policy covers all possible disasters, only those which are listed in it *(though 'all risks' policies work differently – see p. 95)*
- no claims can be paid if the policyholder is in breach of any of his obligations under the policy
- policyholders should read their policies on receipt to see if they provide the expected cover.

This chapter therefore looks in particular at those aspects of insurance which demand a 'buyer beware' attitude. It doesn't consider any types of insurance which fall within the scope of the Financial Services Act – in other words investment-type life insurance; these are dealt with in Chapters 6 to 8.

Basic rules

There are a few general rules to bear in mind when considering insurance. They may prevent your being out of pocket or getting locked into a dispute with your insurance company when you make a claim.

- Get quotes from several different companies. A broker can save you some leg-work (see opposite).
- Never choose an insurance company just because its policies seem cheap. Check that the cover meets your needs and use surveys such as those in *Which?* magazine to see how people who've used the company rate its service.
- Never rely on just a brochure for details of the cover. Ask for a copy of the policy.
- Always read the policy before you buy. Ask the company (or your insurance adviser) to explain anything you're unclear about.
- Make sure you understand phrases such as 'all in' and 'all risks'. Some policies cover only what's actually listed on your policy, others list only what's excluded.
- Watch out for policy 'excesses'. An excess is the first part of any claim which you must pay yourself – insurers use them to discourage small claims. For example, if your policy has a £100 excess, then you'll have to pay the first £100 yourself on claims over £100 and the full cost with smaller claims. Sometimes excesses apply only to certain parts of a policy, such as theft claims. Excesses may be compulsory, in which case you have no choice but to pay them, or they may be voluntary. You usually pay a lower premium if you agree to a voluntary excess.

Finding insurance

Having decided that you need a particular type of insurance, it's a good idea to do a bit of homework to find out what broad sorts of policies are available – the sections on each type of insurance in this chapter will help you do this. Decide what sort of policy would best suit your needs. The next step is to get in touch with someone who offers it.

The direct route

If you know which company you want to go to – either from surveys you've read, say, or because you've dealt with the company before and are happy to use it again – you can contact the company direct and ask to be sent a copy of the policy, a quotation, and the paperwork for taking out a policy. You should ideally contact two or three other companies as well so that you can compare policies and premiums and choose whichever is best.

Using a broker or other intermediary

Alternatively, you could get a broker or other intermediary to sift through what's on the market and find a suitable deal for you. If you want cover through an insurer which is a member of Lloyd's, you'll *have* to use a broker. If you use an intermediary, make sure you still get and read a copy of the policy before making any decisions. (If the intermediary is slow or unwilling to supply a copy of the policy, consider changing to another intermediary.)

Intermediaries often don't look at the full range of companies available, and some are tied to just a handful of companies. So make sure you find out the status of the intermediary you go to and contact two or three and compare the recommendations that you get.

There are all sorts of insurance intermediaries – advisers, consultants, agents and so on – but only *registered* brokers can use the term 'broker'. Brokers must abide by a code of conduct and should give independent advice based on the full range of policies on the market. They must have professional indemnity (PI) insurance which will protect you against loss if they are negligent or go bust. In addition, they are covered by a 'grants scheme' which may help if for some reason the broker's insurance won't pay out.

From 1989, other intermediaries, if they sell the insurance of companies which belong to the Association of British Insurers (ABI), must display a certificate saying that they'll abide by a new code of conduct which the ABI has drawn up, and they must have PI insurance to the same level as registered brokers, though there's no grants scheme or compensation fund. The insurance company (or companies) will be responsible for the action of intermediaries who act as their agents, but not those of independent intermediaries. And intermediaries who sell the policies of non-ABI companies won't have to abide by the code.

You can find a broker or other insurance intermediary by looking in Yellow Pages. And you can get a list of brokers in your area by contacting:

British Insurance and Investment Brokers Association
BIIBA House, 14 Bevis Marks, London EC3A 7NT
Tel: 01-623 9043

TIP *A broker or other intermediary can be particularly useful if you have unusual or difficult insurance needs – for example, if you want life cover but your health is poor, or house insurance for a thatched home.*

The proposal form

Having found the policy you want, the next step is to fill out a proposal form. This is the application form for a particular policy and it will ask you for all sorts of details which the insurer needs in order to decide whether or not to cover you and how much to charge. Care taken at this stage can prevent problems later.

The length of a proposal form and the questions asked varies from one type of insurance to another, and from one company to another. Perhaps the key feature is the declaration that you usually have to sign at the end confirming that the answers are true and that no 'material fact' has been left out. A 'material fact' is anything which the insurer would want to take account of in making a contract with you. You are in the tricky – and somewhat unfair – position of having to read the insurer's mind to decide what they might consider 'material'. And if you fail to disclose something which does turn out to be material, the whole insurance contract could be void. In practice, most insurers would refuse to pay out on a claim only if the undisclosed material fact was relevant to the particular claim – for example, a permanent health insurer might refuse to pay out if you became disabled through taking part in winter sports and you hadn't told them that this was something you did from time to time.

A few insurers have revised their proposal forms and now ask you only to give the information specifically asked for on the form; as long as you answer those questions fully and truthfully, you don't need to volunteer any other details about yourself. But most insurers still have the 'material facts' statement and you'll have to tell them about anything that could be relevant – if you're unsure about whether to disclose something, err on the side of caution and tell the insurer anyway.

WARNING *Be very careful if a broker or other intermediary fills in the proposal form on your behalf. Read what has been written before you sign it and make sure all the facts are exactly as you stated. It is always preferable to fill in the form yourself.*

House buildings insurance

What it covers

You're covered for damage to the building itself, permanent fittings (such as central heating and built-in cupboards), outbuildings, drives, walls and fences. These policies tend to be very similar in the risks that they cover you against. Typically, they'll include: damage by fire, lightning, explosion, earthquake, theft, riot and malicious persons, storm and flood, aircraft and things falling from them, subsidence, landslip and heave, impact by falling trees or vehicles or animals, breakage or collapse of radio and TV aerials, escape of water from tanks and pipes and oil escaping from fixed heating installations, damage to cables or underground service pipes supplying your property. Cover for accidental breakage of glass or damage to lavatories or washbasins may be included or, with some policies, is extra. Individual policies have exclusions (such as damage to gates and fences by frost, storm or flood), so it's important to compare one policy with another.

If you live in a block of flats or a tenement property, you should check your lease to see where your insurance responsibilities lie.

Types of policy

There are two basic sorts of buildings policy: 'standard' ones will cover only specified disasters; 'all risks' policies cover *any* accident except those which are specifically excluded. With a standard policy, you can usually add on 'accidental damage' insurance which will bring the level of cover broadly up to that provided by an all-risks policy and bring the cost to about the same level too.

There are also two sorts of cover: 'indemnity', and 'new-for-old'. 'Indemnity' cover means that the insurer will pay the cost of repairing

CASE HISTORY

Mr and Mrs W put in a substantial claim with their insurance company when they noticed several large cracks developing in part of their house, but the company denied liability. The company's loss adjusters declared that most of the subsidence had occurred two years before the policy was taken out and that some repair work had been carried out, probably shortly after the war, since when the house had been insured with a number of insurers.

Mr and Mrs W got their insurance broker to contact the previous insurers but they too denied liability on the grounds that nothing had been reported to them while their policy was current.

The Ws decided to persist with their claim and eventually succeeded with the first company.

Moral: if you are considering changing your insurance company, it may be a good idea to have a limited structural survey carried out before you switch.

the damage or replacing the item only after making a deduction for wear and tear – so, for example, if an old roof had to be replaced, you'd usually have to pay part of the cost yourself. In most cases you would be wise to go for 'new-for-old' cover instead. 'New-for-old' means you get the full cost of repairs or replacement, though there might be an excess (see p. 92). And insurers won't pay out for damage due to poor maintenance – usually one of the policy conditions is that you'll take reasonable care to keep your property in 'efficient condition and repair'.

What influences cost?

The cost of the insurance depends on the rebuilding cost of your property (see p. 98). The main influences on rebuilding cost are the type of home you have – flat, detached house, bungalow, and so on – the age of the property, its size, and whereabouts you live (because building costs vary from area to area).

One or two companies provide insurance cover based on the size, age and location of the property rather than on rebuilding costs.

Points to note

- If you leave your home unoccupied for more than a set period of time (usually 30 days), the insurance company will not pay, after that time, for any damage under specified sections of the policy.
- Damage by vermin is usually excluded – that can mean rats or squirrels gnawing at electric cables (though damage due to a fire caused by the damaged cables normally would be covered). Similarly, damage by insects or fungus, or caused by condensation, is also generally not covered.
- Locks come under a buildings policy – because they're part of the fixtures and fittings. A lock damaged through burglary or fire would come into the insured perils category, but if you lost your keys, thus rendering the lock useless, no damage would have been caused to the lock so you would have to bear the cost of replacement. Some insurance companies offer cover specifically for replacing external door and window locks, even when the keys have been lost, not stolen.

BUYING INSURANCE

How much to insure for

Getting your sums correct when deciding how much insurance to take out can be one of the biggest factors in getting any claim processed satisfactorily. The sum insured may be based on the householder's own estimate, or – more often – on a mortgage valuer's estimate. If this is too low, the insurance company will not pay more, and will also scale down smaller claims. The effect of this is that in a total loss – for example, if the property burned down – your under-insurance could result in a settlement which was less than the amount needed to rebuild the house.

The market value of your home is no guide as to the amount you should insure it for. The sum insured must be based on the full rebuilding costs including central heating, double glazing, kitchen and bathroom fittings and so on, as well as the cost involved in demolition, clearing the debris, paying fees to professionals and so on.

Your insurer, or insurance intermediary, will provide you with a guide to working out how much cover you need – and an intermediary should be willing to do the calculation for you. There are also two free leaflets:

A Guide to Buildings Insurance from:
Royal Institution of Chartered Surveyors
12 Great George Street, Parliament Square, London SW1P 3AD
Tel: 01-222 7000

Buildings Insurance for Homeowners from:
Association of British Insurers
Aldermary House, 10–15 Queen Street, London EC4N 1TT
Tel: 01-248 4477

These give examples of rebuilding costs for all kinds of properties (detached, old, new, big, small and so on). However, these figures give only what is described as a 'reasonable' guide. If you have a particularly large property, or if it has an unusual feature such as a thatched roof or a round tower, consult one – or preferably two – professional surveyors for a written estimate of the rebuilding costs.

If you have a mortgage, the lender will normally ask the surveyor to give an estimate of the rebuilding cost and the lender will then insist that you're insured for at least that amount.

Whatever figure you decide to insure for, it's important to make sure it's 'index-linked'. This means that the sum is automatically increased each year to keep pace with increased costs of house building. This won't take into account any increase in value in your home due to adding on an extra bedroom, say, or installing central heating. Report any changes like this to the insurance company.

House contents insurance

What it covers

You generally get cover for all the movable possessions you and your family normally keep in your home, including furniture, household items, clothing, and so on, and possessions kept in outbuildings, such as garden tools kept in the shed. The risks you're covered against are similar to those which apply to house buildings insurance (see p. 95).

Types of policy

There are two basic kinds of policy – 'standard' and 'all risks'. Standard policies cover only specified events. All-risks policies cover any accident unless it's specifically excluded.

All-risks policies are generally expensive compared with standard policies (anything from £2 to £20 more for each £1,000 of cover depending on where you live).

A cheaper option is to take out a standard policy but add an all-risks extension to cover specific items or groups of items that you regularly take out of the house – for example, clothing, jewellery, cameras and so on. There's usually a limit on the amount that can be paid out for any one item. You're covered against loss or damage anywhere in the UK and, with most policies, abroad for a limited time (often up to 60 days). There may be an excess (see p. 92) when you claim. Items covered by an all-risks extension don't need to be included in the standard policy cover.

Another option is to add an accidental damage extension on to a standard policy (with or without an all-risks extension), so that if, for example, a carpet is stained, the insurance company will pay up. There's usually an excess and some fragile items, such as glassware, might be excluded.

There are also two types of cover: 'indemnity' and 'new-for-old'. 'Indemnity' means that the insurer deducts an amount for wear and tear from the amounts paid out; 'new-for-old' means that you can claim the full price of replacing or repairing an item. But, even with a new-for-old policy, certain items such as clothes and linen may get only indemnity cover. A new-for-old policy will cost you more than an indemnity policy – anything from £1 to £16 more for each £1,000 of cover – but the extra cost is usually worth it, because indemnity cover only could leave you badly out of pocket if you had to make a substantial claim. A further option is to have an indemnity policy which covers some things – for example, everything up to three years old – on a new-for-old basis. These policies aren't as good as the full new-for-old cover and usually don't cost very much less.

The best choice of house contents insurance for most people is a standard new-for-old policy, with an all-risks extension for possessions regularly taken out of the house.

What influences cost?

The main influence is where you live. Insurers divide the country into areas of higher and lower risk according to their experience of paying out on claims. Busy urban areas where the chance of theft is greater attract the highest premiums, quiet rural areas the lowest.

Points to note

- If you live in a 'high risk' area where theft is a fairly common occurrence and leave the house unoccupied every day, some insurers will charge you much higher premiums or insist on extra security.
- Some policies include a section giving cover for freezer contents if there is a mechanical breakdown or a power cut. If not, you might be able to add this cover for an extra cost (around £1 to £4 for £100 of cover).
- Taking in a lodger can reduce your theft cover to breaking-and-entering only. You might be able to increase the cover by paying extra.
- New-for-old cover is not always precisely what you get. It actually applies only where something is lost or stolen, or totally destroyed, or damaged to an extent that it is utterly beyond repair. If the damage to something is only slight, the insurer might insist it's repaired.
- If only one of a set – for example, one of a pair of earrings – is lost, damaged or stolen, you may be paid only for one, even though you need the pair to get any use out of them. Three-piece suites can

cause problems: some companies look on a suite as a single item for insurance purposes while others say that it consists of three separate items. The Ombudsman has given the view that a policyholder is *not* entitled to a new suite just because one chair is damaged. But some insurers will pay for an entire suite to be recovered, while others may give an *ex gratia* payment (in other words they pay but admit no liability).

How much to insure for

As with buildings cover, don't under-insure your house contents. Go round every room in the house (and outbuildings) and add up what it would cost to replace everything. If you're taking out new-for-old cover, check current prices in the shops.

Make sure your policy is index-linked. If you buy any expensive new items for your home, increase your contents cover as soon as possible – don't wait until renewal.

Car insurance

Types of policy and what they cover

Road Traffic Act cover Everyone who owns and drives a car on the public road must by law have at least basic insurance cover. The absolute minimum (sometimes known as Road Traffic Act cover) must cover your liability for injuries to other people, their property, and their cars, caused by the use of your car while it is on a public road.

Third party, fire and theft cover This incorporates the legal minimum and also covers damage to your own car if it is stolen or burnt. However, it gives no cover if your car is damaged in an accident.

Comprehensive cover This type of cover is the most expensive kind because it covers the widest range of risks. As well as third party, fire and theft, it covers you for damage caused to your car by most other means – so accidents are covered (whoever is at fault), as is damage caused by falling trees and suchlike. The contents of your car – rugs, clothing, carrycot or whatever – are also covered, but there is usually an overall limit. Some policies include extras like paying for your car to be towed away after an accident.

What influences cost?

The main factors are the area in which you live – for example, you'll pay more if you live and drive in a crowded urban area than if you live out in the country – and the type of car that you drive – some cars are more likely to be involved in accidents or more expensive to repair. Age is also important – younger drivers are higher risks and are charged more. Some companies give favourable terms to 'mature' (50+) drivers. There are many other factors which insurers consider such as whether you use your car for business, and your occupation.

Points to note

- The more people allowed to drive your car, the more you'll have to pay in insurance premiums, particularly if anyone is under 25. It might be cheaper for younger drivers to buy an older car, rather than share yours.
- If you don't have a garage but leave your car in the street in a high-risk area, you might not be covered against some risks, and you might be charged more. It might be cheaper in the long run to rent a lock-up garage and pay less to your insurer. If your car is normally kept in a low-risk area but you intend to visit a high-risk area and leave the car on the street overnight, check whether your cover will be reduced.
- Some companies give a discount for older cars, such as those over three years old or five years old – the discount could be anything up to 20 per cent.
- Some insurers charge lower premiums for women because on average they have a better claims record.
- You can reduce your premiums by building up a 'no claims discount' (NCD – sometimes called a 'no claims bonus'). With most companies you get the maximum discount after four years without a claim. If you do make a claim you lose part of the discount unless you have a 'protected NCD' policy which lets you make one or two claims within, say, a five-year period without losing any NCD.
- You can reduce your premiums if you agree to take out a 'voluntary excess' (see p. 92). Watch out for compulsory excesses – for example, if a young person's driving
- Be wary of the words 'any driver' – this doesn't literally mean 'anyone'. The proposal form will have asked various questions

CASE HISTORY

Mr N had a comprehensive policy covering 'any driver' so he wasn't particularly concerned when his brother-in-law borrowed his car and had an accident. But he soon got worried when his insurer refused to pay the £150 claim for damage to his car.

Mr N was appalled to discover that his brother-in-law wasn't covered under the 'any driver' policy because he had been convicted of a drink-driving offence two years previously, which meant that he was driving uninsured when the accident happened. So Mr N had to pay for the repairs. In addition, three pedestrians were injured in the accident and Mr N was faced with the possibility of having to pay for their injury claims – around £5,000.

The insurance company said that Mr N should have checked with them that it was all right to lend the car to his brother-in-law beforehand. They would have told him that the company did not insure drivers with drink-driving convictions.

Moral: consult your insurance company if drivers are young, inexperienced, or have a motoring offence, before handing over the keys.

about intended drivers (whether any have convictions, physical infirmities, and so on). It's up to you to check that people you let drive your car don't fall into these categories, or to inform the insurer that they do, *before* you let the person drive your car. Claims have been refused because, previously unknown to the insurer, another driver had a conviction for drink-driving.

How much to insure for

Go for the kind of policy best suited to both your car and your pocket. Your brand new, fairly new, or old but very expensive car deserves comprehensive cover. But if you run an old banger for which major repairs wouldn't make sense because of the cost compared to the value of the car, third party, fire and theft may be the sensible choice.

Life insurance

What it covers

Term – or 'protection-only' This type of insurance pays out if you die within a set period of time – the 'term'. If you survive the term it pays out nothing. It can be arranged on the lives of two people – for example, a married couple – to pay out when one or both of you has died.

Investment-type insurance – such as endowment and whole life policies – accumulates a surrender value which may be paid out on death, when the policy matures or when it is cashed in. Though these policies include a protection element, their main use is for investment purposes and they are covered in Chapters 6 to 8, not here.

Types of term insurance policy

Lump sum policies This is the basic term insurance. It pays out a set lump sum if you die within the term.

Family income benefit (FIB) policies Basic FIB policies pay out a fixed monthly income if you die within the term. The income is paid from the time you die until the end of the term, and is tax-free. Because the amount the policy must pay out falls as the term left to run falls, these policies are cheaper than equivalent lump sum policies and are a particularly good deal for people with young families.

Whether you choose a lump sum or an FIB policy there are variations, which are described below. Often, you can combine the different elements to produce, say, a 'renewable increasing term insurance'.

Increasing term insurance The amount of cover is automatically increased at regular intervals either by a set amount or in line with inflation. Premiums are higher than for a level cover policy but often are the same throughout the whole term. Most people should consider this type of policy to lessen the impact of inflation on the level of cover.

Increasable term insurance At set dates throughout the term (such as the policy anniversary) you choose whether or not to increase the cover. If you increase the cover, your premium rises but there's no weighting for any deterioration in your health. This can be a useful option where, say, you expect to want to increase your cover as you have more children.

Decreasing term insurance The amount of cover reduces during the term. Often used as a 'mortgage protection policy' to cover a repayment mortgage (see p. 48) and pay off the amount of the outstanding loan if you die within the mortgage term. Can also be used to protect other loans.

Renewable term insurance At the end of the term you have the option to take out further term insurance. The premiums for the new policy are not weighted for any deterioration in your health. This can be a useful option.

Convertible term insurance You have the option to convert the policy into another kind of life insurance. Premiums for the new type of policy might take account of any change in health.

What influences cost?
You'll pay more the older you are and the poorer your health. Women usually pay less than men of the same age because they have a greater life expectancy.

Points to note
- If what you need is just protection for your dependants, take out term insurance – for example, an increasing family income benefit policy. Don't take out investment-type insurance – it's expensive.
- If you've suffered from some serious illness – had a heart by-pass operation, for example – finding life insurance may be difficult. Try going to a broker.
- If you don't smoke, consider companies which give a special discount to non-smokers – but always check that another insurer isn't offering cheaper rates regardless of whether or not you smoke.
- The emergence of AIDS has made some insurance companies increase their premiums (some just for men of a particular age group, others for men of any age, others for single men of specified age groups and still others for both sexes). Some policies allow for premiums to be increased during the term. Shopping around is essential.

How much to insure for

This will vary enormously depending on your particular circumstances. Work out what your dependants' needs would be – mortgage, regular bills, household spending, running a car, replacing the car if yours is a company one, and so on. Deduct any help they'd get from the state and any savings due to, say, the fact that you are no longer commuting. Are you in an insurance scheme through your job? Many employers run such schemes, often as part of the pension scheme. If there's a shortfall between the spending needs you've calculated and the income that would come in, you need to take out life insurance.

If you have children and they're being looked after by your partner, you'll probably need insurance on your partner's life too to cover the cost of, say, a nanny or a nursery place. You might want to cover the cost of help round the house too – a cleaning lady, gardener, even a cook.

You'll have to decide whether to choose a lump sum or an FIB policy. FIB policies are generally cheaper, but they're less flexible.

Permanent health insurance

What it covers

This type of insurance gives you a monthly income if you are ill and unable to work, right up to retirement age if necessary. Most policies won't pay out if you're off work because of self-inflicted injuries, alcohol, non-prescribed drugs, pregnancy (unless you're incapacitated owing to complications after three months), or war. Most policies also exclude claims due to AIDS.

Types of policy

Level (flat rate) cover and income With these the amount of cover you have does not change. And, if you're ill and receiving an income from the policy, the amount of income doesn't change either.

Increasing cover and income With these policies, both the amount of cover you take out before you are ill and the amount of income paid out while you are ill increase either by a fixed amount or in line with inflation.

Increasing cover *or* income Some policies increase only the amount of cover you have before you are ill. Others increase only the income you get while you are ill.

What influences cost?

PHI is fairly expensive. Premiums will increase with your age and with poor health. Women usually have to pay higher premiums than men. You may pay less if you're in a 'low-risk' job such as teaching, more if you're in a 'high-risk' job such as building work.

Points to note

- If you are self-employed this type of insurance could be essential. It could be your major source of income since state sickness benefits provide only a very low income.
- The index-linked or increasing type of policy is more expensive, but if you take out only a level policy it would be worth just over half as much in ten years' time, assuming an inflation rate of five per cent a year over the period.
- There's a time-lag between the start of your illness and time the policy starts to pay out – the 'deferment' period. You can choose anything from a month to two years' deferment. The longer the deferment period the less you pay in premiums. Consider whether you're able or prepared to dig into your savings, and, if so, for how long.
- Check the policy carefully for any restrictions on risky hobbies and establish what the insurer considers these to be. Also look out for restrictions related to your living abroad for any length of time.
- If you're a non-smoker you can get a lower premium from some insurers. But check that you can't get an even cheaper premium with another company that doesn't make this distinction.

How much to insure for

This depends very much on your personal circumstances. Most policies put certain limits on the amount you can get. For example, you can't usually take out cover for more than three-quarters of your earnings, and with some companies the limit is just a half of earnings. There will probably be a deduction too to take account of any state benefits that you qualify for. Some companies reduce the amount of cover on earnings above a particular level.

Private medical insurance

What it covers

This type of insurance pays your bills when you are treated by a medical specialist to whom you've been referred by your GP or dentist (but you don't need to be referred if you end up in hospital in an emergency). It includes hospital accommodation, nursing charges, surgeons' and anaesthetists' fees, X-rays, drugs, radiotherapy, chemotherapy, home nursing you may be recommended to have and any out-patient or day care you may need.

Types of policy

Basically, there are two types of policy. One gives you the option of having medical consultations and any hospital treatment privately instead of through the National Health Service. The option can be exercised at any time to suit you.

The other option enables you to have private treatment only if the NHS cannot provide it within a certain time (eg six weeks) of your seeing an NHS consultant.

What influences cost?

The type of hospital you choose will affect the cost (there are often three different price bands) and different parts of Britain have different fees for these. In most cases premiums will increase with age. Married couples usually have to pay less than two single people, and children may be able to be included at special family rates. You may be able to get a discount if you belong to a 'group': for instance, your trade association or professional body may have negotiated a discount with one of the insurers.

Points to note

- You won't be covered for all medical treatment. One very important exclusion is any health problem which you already knew about before buying a policy or indeed problems that you had in the past.
- Other things not covered include, for instance, pregnancy care or labour (although problems arising from pregnancy or labour may be covered). Infertility and associated treatment are also excluded

from many policies, as are abortion and vasectomy, unless carried out on medical grounds.

- While you won't be covered for an incurable illness, you may be covered for relief of an acute phase of the illness.
- Private treatment doesn't necessarily mean treatment in a private hospital. You can get private treatment in an NHS hospital and benefit from NHS facilities and back-up services. You'll get a private room but this may not always mean a single one – you might have to share.
- Policies all have different limits and restrictions. These could relate to the amount of out-patient treatment or home nursing you're covered for, or you may find that the surgeon charges more for an operation than the policy will pay.

How much to insure for
Be careful about getting too little cover: some policies have an overall limit on the amount each person can claim in one year, while others have limits on one particular aspect of care, such as surgeons' fees. Others have no limits on any type of cover.

Holiday insurance

What it covers
You and your belongings while you are on holiday and travelling there and back. Typical cover includes medical expenses, cancellation or cutting short your holiday due to illness, jury service, redundancy or some types of domestic crisis (for example, if your house is badly damaged by fire or burgled), loss or damage to your belongings, loss of money or travellers cheques, a limited amount to spend if your baggage is delayed or you are delayed, personal liability for injury you cause to someone else or damage you cause to their property.

Types of policy
An 'inclusive' policy will cover all the items above. You might be able to get a 'selective' policy where you choose which items of cover you want – but these tend to work out expensive.

If you're intending to engage in dangerous sports such as skiing or parascending, you'll need special insurance to cover the extra risks.

What influences cost?

Where you are going and how much cover you choose.

Points to note

- If you're taking out your insurance through the tour operator, the information you get about the policy is often covered only briefly on the back page of the holiday brochure. Make sure you know exactly what the conditions are and, more importantly, the exclusions. The brochures always tell you how you can obtain full policy details.

- Some tour operators insist that you take out the insurance that they've arranged. This practice is legal, and at present the only thing you can do if you're not happy with the policy is to book your holiday through another operator.

- If you find a travel agent pushing you to take out a policy instead of, or in addition to, the tour operator's, don't assume that it's a better policy. Remember that agents get paid commission on the policies they manage to sell to customers. From time to time there have been problems with holidaymakers being sold inadequate insurance this way, so read through thoroughly any policy you're offered.

- Don't rely on the reciprocal health agreement the UK has with the EC countries and some other countries. It's a useful back-up but has severe limitations.

- Look for policies which include a 24-hour medical emergency service. Make sure it's an English-speaking service that you can call on.

- Watch out for the condition which excludes 'hazardous activities'. For example, this can mean riding a hired moped or water-skiing. Get a written statement from your insurers as to how they view them when it comes to paying out on claims. And if you know you intend to take part in such activities arrange extra insurance.

- Some insurers won't pay claims resulting from pregnancy at all; others won't pay if you were pregnant when you took out the policy, or if you'll be in the last two months or so of pregnancy when you travel.

- Check your house contents insurance to see what cover it gives while your belongings are away from home. You may find it covers everything, or at least valuable items, removing or reducing your need for baggage cover under your holiday insurance.

- Contact lenses are not usually covered. In many cases the same applies to camera lenses, since they are considered 'fragile'. Check whether they are or could be covered by your house contents insurance.
- If a policy allows for cancellation of your holiday in the case of the illness or death of a close relative or business associate, beware of the general phrase used to describe that – 'unforeseen circumstances'. If the relative or business associate was even only slightly ill when you took over the policy the insurer might argue that there was always a possibility of their taking a turn for the worse, and therefore refuse to pay up. If relevant to you, check whether there's a limit on the age of the relative – sometimes the age limit is, for example, 75.
- If you have a medical complaint which you know about when you take out insurance, you can often still get insurance cover, providing you are not travelling against your doctor's orders or going abroad for medical treatment.
- If you've got children, look out for those policies which give good discounts for them.
- Holidaying abroad by car means you need cover not just for yourself and family, but for the car too. Consult your normal car insurer – you can usually get your car insurance extended to cover the trip.

How much to insure for

You should always check the limits under each section of a policy to make sure they are adequate. For example, if you're going to the USA, sufficient cover for medical expenses is essential – £1,000,000 isn't too much. Remember that some items may be covered by your house contents insurance (see p. 99).

Complaints about insurance

If you're unhappy about the way your policy or claim is handled, you should first complain to the company. If you used a broker or other intermediary, they might help you make your complaint. If the ordinary staff can't help, take your complaint to the manager of the branch you deal with. If you're still not happy, write to the head office of the company. If you don't have a contact, address your letter to the Complaints Manager, or phone first and ask who deals with complaints.

Alternatively, libraries keep directories listing the top officials in a company, together with the address of the head office.

If the company can't resolve the complaint to your satisfaction, you can take it to the Insurance Ombudsman, if the company is a member of this scheme – see p. 158 for further information. If the company doesn't belong to the Ombudsman scheme, it might be a member of the Personal Insurance Advisory Service, which can also act in the case of disputes.

Complaints concerning a registered broker should be taken up with the broker first, taking the complaint to the highest level in the firm if necessary. If you're still not satisfied, you could complain to:

Insurance Brokers Registration Council
15 St Helen's Place, London EC3 6DS
Tel: 01-588 4387

Alternatively, you could contact one of the relevant trade bodies if the broker is a member, for example:

British Insurance and Investment Brokers Association (BIIBA)
BIIBA House, 14 Bevis Marks, London EC3A 7NT
Tel: 01-623 9043

Institute of Insurance Consultants (IIC)
PO Box 381, 121a Queensway, Bletchley, Milton Keynes,
Buckinghamshire MK1 1XZ
Tel: 0908 643364

If your complaint concerns a Lloyd's broker, contact:

Lloyd's Consumer Enquiries Department
Lloyd's, 1 Lime Street, London EC3M 7DQ
Tel: 01-623 7100

If your complaint is with another type of intermediary, check whether they are displaying an ABI certificate showing that they are covered by the ABI Code of Conduct (see p. 93). If they are and they are tied agents of one or more insurance companies, you could take your complaint to one of these insurers if the intermediary has been unable to settle the matter. Alternatively, you could contact:

Association of British Insurers
Aldermary House, 10–15 Queen Street, London EC4N 1TT
Tel: 01-248 4477

If the intermediary is not covered by the Code, check the notepaper used by them in any correspondence to see whether it displays the name or logo of a trade body, such as the IIC (see opposite). If it does, try taking your complaint to them.

If you end up losing money because the insurance company you're claiming against goes bust, you may be able to get up to 90 per cent of any reasonable claim back through a compensation scheme set up under the Policyholders' Protection Act – see p. 165 for further details.

6

Saving and investing

Never invest your money in anything that eats or needs repairing. Billy Rose

If you're looking for a home for your savings or investments, you probably feel spoilt for choice. Every kind of financial institution, from building societies to unit trusts, from banks to insurance companies is competing for your attention and your money. But you need different investments according to your needs and your circumstances. So once you take a closer look, the choice of appropriate investment probably is narrower than it might at first appear.

Sound foundations

Before considering other uses for your 'spare' money, you should ensure that your financial foundation is sound. This means taking steps to cover yourself in case of emergency and planning ahead.

An emergency fund

You should make sure that part of your money is speedily available in case of sudden need – for example, if you need costly repairs to keep your car on the road, the roof springs a leak, or you suddenly have to visit far-flung relatives in a family crisis. The money must be invested where you can get at it whenever needed but where it will still earn a reasonable return. The best place is likely to be an interest-earning account with a building society or bank, possibly with a large cash machine network. The amount you need will depend partly on your access to credit – if, say, you have a high limit on your credit card *and* a large part of the limit is usually unused, you might not need much in your emergency fund. For many people, around £500 to £1,000 in an emergency fund would be enough.

Protecting your family

If you have dependants – children, or a dependent parent perhaps – you should ensure that they'd be financially protected if you, or your husband or wife, were to die. For most people this means taking out life insurance. If it's protection that you need, avoid expensive investment-type life insurance; instead, choose protection-only (term) insurance (see p. 104 for details). If you're self-employed, or if your employer doesn't run a suitable scheme, consider whether you'd need to replace your earnings if you were ill for a long time or permanently disabled. If you would, then you need permanent health insurance (see p. 106).

Your home

You need to live somewhere, and buying your own home might double up as a sound investment. Big profits have been made in the housing market in the past, but there's no guarantee that will continue. Most people can't afford to buy a home outright so need a mortgage – see p. 44.

Pension

You may be tempted to put off retirement planning until you're older, but it takes a long time to build up enough to provide a good pension so pension saving should start as early as possible. If you belong to a pension scheme through your job, you might think there's no need for you to do anything, but you should consider whether you need to make extra contributions, and whether or not to stay in part of the state pension scheme. If you're self-employed, you should contribute to a personal plan. (For information about pension planning, see the *Which?* action pack, *Choose Your Pension*, available from Consumers' Association, PO Box 44, Hertford SG14 1LH, price £7.95.)

Basic investment strategy

How long can you invest?

If you need to get at your money easily, or might need it back at short notice, avoid investments where you have to give a long period of notice before you can withdraw your money (for example, building society 90-day notice accounts), or where there are penalties if you want your money back too soon (for example, many types of life insurance). Don't commit yourself to regular savings schemes if you're not sure that you can keep up the payments – choose a more flexible investment where you can save varying amounts at irregular intervals.

How much risk can you take?

In general terms, you need to take on more risk for the chance of a higher return. There are three main types of risk:

- losing capital. With investments such as shares (including investments linked to shares – for example, unit trusts and unit-linked life insurance), the amount of your investment can fall as well as rise, as the market price of the shares falls and rises. This means that you can't be sure of any profits until you've actually withdrawn them, and that at times your investment could quite easily be worth less than you'd originally invested. This is not the home for money that you might need back at short notice – perhaps when prices are low. But to stand the chance of a good return over the long term, you'll generally need to put at least some of your money into investments of this type

- losing interest. Some investments, such as most building society shares and accounts, offer a rate of interest which will go up and down in line with the general level of interest rates. This might be a problem if you need a reasonably steady income – something like British Government stocks might be more suitable. Some other investments, such as National Savings Certificates or insurance-type income or growth bonds, offer a return which is fixed at the time you invest. This can be useful, but of course if interest rates on other investments rise, you'll have lost out. If interest rates on other investments fall, you'll be relatively better off
- inflation. With some investments – for example, building society accounts and National Savings deposits – your money earns interest but the amount you originally invested – your capital – doesn't grow. The problem here is that even a modest rate of inflation will eat seriously into the buying power of your money. For example, just five per cent a year inflation would reduce the buying power of £1,000 to £952 after one year, £784 after five years and just £614 after ten years. And the buying power of the income from the investment will be eroded in a similar way. A few investments – for example, index-linked National Savings Certificates and index-linked British Government stocks – protect your money against inflation, though you will have to accept a lower return in the short term. But for most long-term savers or for people relying on income from their investments (during retirement, say), at least some of your money should probably be in investments where your capital can grow and hopefully keep abreast of inflation.

It's impossible to know in advance which are going to be the worst risks to take – you can't predict with any accuracy a major stock market crash, a period of runaway inflation, or a nosedive in interest rates, though you can be fairly sure they'll all come to pass if you invest for long enough. The best strategy is to choose a mix of investments with different balances of risk and return to form an investment portfolio which overall reflects the amount of risk you feel comfortable with.

TIP *Never put all your financial eggs in one basket. Spread your savings across a mix of investments.*

This strategy also extends to most investments of one type. Suppose, for example, you invest some of your money in shares. Putting a lot of money into the shares of just one company would be a high risk strategy – bad profits or a strike, say, could topple the share price. If you buy the shares of several companies, then a fall in the share price of one of them will affect only part of your investment – spreading your money will reduce your exposure to that risk. Similarly, consider spreading your investment across shares in companies in more than one sector – some in oil companies, some in food companies, some in electronics, and so on – and perhaps more than one country. Similarly, if you invest in unit trusts or investment-type life insurance, say, it's a good idea to spread your money across several trusts or companies.

WARNING *When an investment offers returns which seem too good to be true and are out of line with returns being offered by similar schemes, the alarm bells should start ringing. Check carefully what risks are involved – extra returns nearly always mean extra risks – and consider whether you want to take them. If no extra risks are apparent, be suspicious – is the scheme above board?*

WARNING *Investors in the UK are now covered by a fairly high standard of protection under the Financial Services Act 1986 (see Chapter 8), though even this has loopholes. But standards of investor protection abroad vary considerably from one country to another. So be very wary of investing with an offshore company. If you want to invest abroad, stick with a UK company which runs UK-based funds or trusts specialising in foreign investments.*

Your tax position

Investments and tax The return you get can be income, capital growth or a combination of both. What's important to you is the *after tax* return that you'll get. The return from some investments is tax-free, but with most the income is subject to income tax and the capital gains are subject to capital gains tax. Whether tax is in fact payable will depend on whether you've used your available allowances and other deductions. So your personal tax position will often make one type of investment more suitable for you than another.

WARNING *Advertisements for offshore investments seem very enticing with talk of* 'income paid gross' *and* 'tax-free'. *But watch out – often it's only the very tiny print which reveals that only non-residents can get these returns and that UK residents will have to pay tax.*

You and tax Everyone, including children, can receive a certain amount of income – whether from earnings or investments or both – before they have to pay any income tax. At the minimum, you'll get the single person's allowance. You'll have a higher allowance if you're a married man, you're 65 or over during the tax year (and have an income below a certain level), or you qualify for one of various other income tax allowances. You can also make various other deductions – called outgoings – from your income before tax becomes payable. Once you've used up your outgoings and allowances, tax is charged at the basic rate, and at a higher rate on any income above a given amount.

You have a tax-free allowance before any tax is due on capital gains. When the allowance is used up, you pay capital gains tax at the same rate as the basic rate of income tax. But if your taxable income plus your taxable gains takes you over a given threshold, tax on part of your gains will be charged at a rate equal to the higher rate of income tax.

Non-taxpayers If you're a non-taxpayer, because you have unused outgoings or allowances, you should normally avoid certain investments where income is paid with tax already deducted and the tax can't be reclaimed. This is the case with most deposit-type investments such as bank and building society accounts, and investment-type life insurance schemes. But always make sure that the before-tax return you can get elsewhere is higher than the taxed return you're giving up. Investments paying income with tax deducted but where you *can* reclaim the tax may not be very convenient and you may have to wait some time before getting the tax back.

TIP *Most children will want to have some savings at least in a bank or building society account giving instant access. However, interest from these accounts is paid with tax deducted which can't be reclaimed, so for children, who have a single person's tax allowance just like any adult, these usually don't offer the best returns. Children can make use of their tax allowance by investing any money not needed in the short* *term in a National Savings Investment Account, where interest is paid without tax deducted. The snag with this account is that one month's notice of withdrawal is required. But watch out whatever account they choose – income from money that a parent gives to their child is taxed as the parent's income, so encourage generous relatives to give money to the children for birthdays, Christmas, and so on.*

Basic rate taxpayers Paying tax on investments is often very simple since, with many, tax at the basic rate has already been deducted when you receive or are credited with income (though you still have to declare it on your tax return). Consider investments which offer a tax-free return if this would be higher than the taxed return from other investments. And, if you're not fully using your capital gains tax allowance, consider investments where the return is in the form of capital gain rather than income.

WARNING *The return from investment-type life insurance is handed to you after tax has been paid by the company, and if you're a basic rate taxpayer there's never any more tax to pay. This is the company's own tax that's been paid; you can't reclaim it. But the tax has come out of the pool of money otherwise available to investors so the company's tax bill is an influence on the return you get. At present, the company's tax is higher than the amount a basic rate taxpayer would otherwise have paid. This means that, other things being equal, you'd be better off investing in, say, unit trusts (where you pay tax directly on the return) than in unit-linked life insurance. From 1 January 1990, it's been proposed that the situation changes slightly. If the proposals (made in the 1989 Budget) become law, insurance companies will then pay tax at a lower rate than now. Basic rate taxpayers with unused capital gains tax allowance might then still do better with other investments, but if you've no unused allowance left, investment-type life insurance could be just as good. The Government is also considering ways of simplifying the way in which tax is paid on life insurance.*

Higher rate taxpayers The 1988 Budget, which cut the top rate of income tax from 60 per cent to 40 per cent and brought the tax rates on capital gains and income into line, has made life much simpler. Your main concern nowadays is to make sure that you make full use of your capital gains tax allowance so as to minimise your total tax bill. Also consider investments offering a tax-free return (such as National Savings Certificates) or largely tax-free return ('low coupon' or index-linked British Government stocks, say). As long as you've used your capital gains tax allowance, consider investment-type life insurance too; with most policies for regular saving, there's no tax for you personally to pay, and the life company will have paid tax at a lower rate than you would have had to otherwise.

Different investments

Below is a summary of the main types of investment available with some pointers on what to watch out for. In the space available it's possible to give no more than an outline of each. (For a complete review, see *Which? Way to Save and Invest* available from bookshops, and from Consumers' Association, Castlemead, Gascoyne Way, Hertford SG14 1LH, price £10.95.)

Deposit (savings) accounts
Where from Building societies, banks, finance houses, National Savings Bank (through post offices).

How they work Subject to any minimum or maximum investments, you pay in whatever you want, whenever you want. The amount of your capital doesn't vary, but earns interest (which is usually added to your account but can be paid out on a regular basis with some accounts). Interest is usually variable and changes with the general level of interest rates in the economy. Some accounts offer higher interest if you have more than a certain amount in your account. You can withdraw your money instantly with some accounts (though you may lose some interest, and there might be a limit on the amount of cash you can withdraw in any one day; with others, you'll have to give notice – 30 days or 90 days, say.

Minimum investment Varies. For example, £1 for many accounts, £5 for National Savings Investment and Ordinary accounts, £250 upwards for 'higher interest' accounts.

Maximum investment Usually none.

Tax National Savings accounts pay interest before tax has been deducted; interest is taxable except the first £70 from an Ordinary account (husband and wife each get £70 tax-free). Building societies, banks and finance houses pay interest after the equivalent of basic rate tax has been deducted – non-taxpayers can't reclaim it, basic rate taxpayers have no more tax to pay, higher rate taxpayers have more tax to pay.

Good for Emergency fund. Odd bits of spare cash. National Savings accounts good for non-taxpayers, including children.

Bad for Committed regular savings or a lump sum you can tie up for a while – you can probably get a better return elsewhere.

TIP *The best returns from deposit-type accounts are often offered by the smaller building societies. But unless there's a branch, or agency, near you, you'll have to weigh the extra interest against the inconvenience of dealing with the account by post.*

WARNING *If you withdraw money from a notice account which has been open for less than the full notice period, you could end up with less money than you originally paid in. For example, with a 90-day notice account, you'll find that the full 90-day interest penalty has been deducted. So don't open an account with a long notice period if there's a risk that you'll need your money back early. And to avoid penalties once the account is past the initial period, make sure you give the notice required, and that you withdraw money on the* exact *day the notice period is completed. If you don't, some societies may insist that you start all over again and give fresh notice of withdrawal or incur the full interest penalty as if you'd given no notice.*

WARNING *Though the first £70 of interest from the National Savings Ordinary account is tax free, the rate of interest is traditionally very low, making this account uncompetitive for most investors. And note that the higher rate quoted for the Ordinary account applies only if you keep the account for at least a year and have a minimum balance of £500 – otherwise, the lower rate applies.*

Regular monthly savings accounts

Where from Banks, building societies, Yearly Plan from the National Savings Certificate and SAYE Office, Yearly Plan Section, Durham DH99 1NS (forms available through post offices)

How they work With most bank and building society schemes, you agree to save a regular monthly amount for at least a year (can be longer). The amount of your capital can't fall and earns interest – the rate can vary. You may be able to make one or two withdrawals a year, but notice – three months, say – is normally required.

Building societies also offer special SAYE schemes; you save a regular monthly amount for five years and earn a fixed return. If you leave the money for a further two years a bonus is added. The return is poor if you cash in before five years is up.

With the National Savings Yearly Plan, you pay a fixed amount each month for a year, and then leave your money invested for a further four years. You earn a fixed return which is reduced if you cash in before five years is up.

Minimum investment SAYE schemes – £1 a month. National Savings Yearly Plan – £20 a month. Other schemes – varies, around £5 a month.

Maximum investment SAYE schemes – £20 a month. National Savings Yearly Plan – £200 a month. Other schemes – varies, around £500 a month.

Tax Returns from SAYE schemes and the National Savings Yearly Plan are tax-free. With other schemes, the return is taxable and paid after the equivalent of basic rate tax has been deducted (and this can't be reclaimed by non-taxpayers).

Good for Imposing the discipline of regular saving. SAYE accounts and National Savings Yearly Plan can be good investments for higher rate taxpayers.

Bad for Anyone who can't commit themselves to regular saving.

National Savings Capital Bonds

Where from National Savings Bank & Capital Bond Office, Glasgow G58 1SB (forms available through post offices)

How they work You invest a lump sum for five years. The amount of your capital can't fall and earns a return which is fixed at the time you invest and which is highest if you hold the bond for the full five years. The return is poor if you withdraw your money early, and three months' notice of withdrawal is required.

Minimum investment £100.

Maximum investment None.

Tax Return is taxable as income but paid without any tax having been deducted.

Good for Depending on interest rate at the time you invest, non-taxpayers who can tie up their money for five years – could be a good gift from a grandparent, say, to a child.

Bad for Anyone who can't tie up their money for five years.

WARNING *Despite its name, the return on a Capital Bond is interest and is subject to income tax. This means that, depending on your tax position, tax may be payable each year on the amount of interest credited to your bond.*

National Savings Income Bonds

Where from National Savings Bonds & Stock Office, Blackpool FY3 9YP (forms available through post offices)

How they work You invest a lump sum. The value of your capital can't fall and earns interest which is paid to you monthly. Withdrawals require three months' notice and must be in multiples of £1,000. If you want your money back within the first year, your rate of interest is halved. You must keep a minimum balance of £2,000 in the bond.

Minimum investment £2,000 and multiples of £1,000 after that.

Maximum investment £100,000.

Tax Interest is taxable as income but paid before any tax has been deducted.

Good for Depending on returns available elsewhere, non-taxpayers who want income and can tie up a lump sum.

Bad for Anyone who can't tie up their money for a year. Taxpayers can probably do better with a building society account.

National Savings Certificates
Where from Post offices, banks.

How they work You invest a lump sum for a return which is fixed at the time you invest. Interest earned increases each year and you get the best return if you can invest for a full five years. If you cash in during the first year, you get back only what you invested.
   A variation is index-linked National Savings Certificates. These are like the ordinary Certificates except that the return you get is linked to inflation measured as changes in the Retail Prices Index, plus a bonus if you keep the Certificates for five years.

Minimum investment £25

Maximum investment Ordinary Certificates – £1,000 (34th issue) plus a further £10,000 if you are re-investing the proceeds from earlier issues. Index-linked Certificates – £5,000.

Tax Tax-free.

Good for Higher rate taxpayers. Basic rate taxpayers who want a relatively safe and simple investment with a fixed lump sum return. Anyone who thinks interest rates might fall. Index-linked Certificates are good for people who think that inflation might take off.

Bad for Anyone who wants ready access to their money.

WARNING *After five years, you can leave your money invested in National Savings Certificates and it continues to earn tax-free interest at the* 'General extension rate'. *This rate is not fixed, and it does not necessarily follow the level of general interest rates. You need to keep an eye on the return you're getting and work out whether you'd be better off investing your money elsewhere.*

TIP *Interest is added to National Savings Certificates at the end of each complete three-month period (starting with the date on which you bought them). This continues even after the five-year fixed-return period is up. If you decide to cash in your Certificates, make sure you do so at the end of an interest period. (This does not apply to index-linked National Savings Certificates which are revalued every month.)*

Insurance company income and growth bonds

Where from Insurance companies, through financial advisers.

How they work You invest a lump sum for a fixed period of time which is different for different bonds – for example, two years or five years. The return is fixed at the time you invest, and either accumulates to be paid out when the bond comes to an end or is paid out regularly as income. You can't usually get your money back early.

Minimum investment Varies, for example £500 or £2,000.

Maximum investment None.

Tax Varies. With all, the return is paid with the equivalent of basic rate tax already deducted. With some, non-taxpayers can reclaim the tax paid, with others they can't. Basic rate taxpayers have no more tax to pay. Higher rate taxpayers may have to pay extra tax. Check the tax position before you invest.

Good for Anyone seeking a fixed return and who can leave their money for a time. Some are useful for non-taxpayers, but check tax position before you invest. People who think interest rates might fall.

Bad for Anyone who might need ready access to their money.

Local authority loans

Where from Local authorities.

How they work You invest a lump sum for a fixed amount of time – anything between one and ten years – and get a fixed rate of interest. Interest is usually paid half-yearly, but with some loans it accumulates and is paid out when the loan comes to an end. If you cash in early, you might not get back the whole of the lump sum you invested.

Minimum investment Varies, for example £500 or £1,000.

Maximum investment Varies.

Tax Interest is paid with the equivalent of basic rate tax deducted. Non-taxpayers can't reclaim the tax.

Good for People who want a fixed and guaranteed return and can tie their money up for at least a year.

Bad for Anyone who might need their money back early. People seeking capital growth.

British Government stocks (gilts)

Where from Stockbrokers or other investment advisers, or the National Savings Stock Register. New issues of stock through newspapers.

How they work You invest a lump sum. You can choose to invest for a fixed time (until 'redemption', though there are a few stocks with no set redemption date) for a fixed return. The return is made up of two parts interest (the 'coupon') and a capital gain (or loss) on redemption. If you don't want to keep your stocks until redemption, you can sell them on the stock market. The amount you get back then depends on the market price of the stock which will rise and fall (depending mainly on the general level of interest rates) – so in this case, your return is not fixed at the time you invest.

A variation is index-linked British Government stocks. These are similar to conventional stocks, but both the income and the amount that you get back at redemption are increased in line with inflation throughout the life of the stock.

Minimum investment In theory none. In practice, dealing costs are disproportionately high if you trade less than, say, £1,500 of stock through a broker or adviser. Use the National Savings Stock Register if you want to buy or sell smaller amounts.

Maximum investment £10,000 a day per stock if you deal through the National Savings Stock Register, otherwise none.

Tax Interest is subject to income tax and is usually paid with basic rate tax already deducted. Non-taxpayers can reclaim the tax already paid. Capital gains are tax-free. If you buy stocks through the National Savings Stock Register (in other words, through the Post Office), interest is paid without tax deducted.

Good for Different stocks have different balances of income and capital gain or loss, so can suit a wide range of investors. People looking for a regular income should choose high coupon stocks. Higher rate taxpayers and anyone seeking tax-free capital gains should consider low coupon stocks. Anyone who wants a fixed return and can leave their money invested. People who can take a chance on movements in the market (by buying and then selling before redemption). Index-linked stocks are good for anyone who needs at least part of their investments to keep pace with inflation, and are good for higher rate taxpayers.

Bad for Anyone who might need their money back at short notice. Index-linked stocks are not suitable for people seeking a high income.

WARNING
Buying and selling British Government stocks through the National Savings Stock Register is cheaper if you are dealing in small amounts. But you have to place your instructions by post which is slower than using a broker or adviser and also means that you don't know in advance the price that you'll buy or sell at.

Local authority bonds
Where from Banks or stockbrokers.

How they work   These are similar to British Government stocks but are issued by local authorities instead of the central government. You invest a lump sum. You can choose to invest until redemption and get a fixed return, or you can sell earlier on the stock market. If you hold to redemption, you get back the same amount that you invested, so your overall return is made up only of interest. If you sell before redemption, what you get back will depend on the market price at the time you sell, and the return is made up of two parts – interest and capital gain (or loss).

Minimum investment   £1,000.

Maximum investment   None.

Tax   Interest is taxable and paid with basic rate income tax already deducted. Non-taxpayers can reclaim the tax. Capital gains are tax-free.

Good for   People seeking a fixed income who can tie their money up. People wanting to take a chance on the stock market.

Bad for   Anyone who might need their money back at short notice.

With-profits insurance policies
Where from   Life insurance companies, life insurance brokers and other investment advisers.

How they work   There are different types of policy. With a regular premium plan, you invest monthly or annually, often for a set period (the 'endowment' period) such as ten years. At the end you get back a lump sum which is made up of a guaranteed sum plus bonuses which have been added. 'Reversionary' bonuses are added at intervals throughout the life of the plan, and a 'terminal' bonus is added when the plan matures. The proceeds of different plans vary enormously – the best performers can give you more than double the worst. The amount of each bonus depends on the general profitability of the insurance company and will be influenced by such things as how well the company's investments perform, its expenses in running its business, distributions to shareholders, if there are any, and so on. Once added, bonuses can't be taken away. But if you want to stop or cash in your plan early there could be early surrender penalties and you might even get back less than you'd invested. 'Whole life' policies do not run for a set period but, as the name suggests, for the whole of your life, though you might not have to carry on paying premiums after a certain age – say, 75. A whole life policy accumulates a 'cash-in value' which can be substantial as the policy ages. But there are usually hefty surrender penalties if you cash in during the early years.

With single premium plans you invest a lump sum which earns bonuses in the same way as regular premium policies. With single premium plans, there is often a facility to enable you to withdraw a regular income.

Minimum investment Varies. Regular premium plans – around £15 a month, say. Single premium plans – around £1,000, say.

Maximum investment None.

Tax Varies according to the type of plan. Most regular premium plans are 'qualifying policies'. With these, there's no tax for you to pay as long as you hold the policy for at least ten years (or three-quarters of its original term if less). If you cash it in early, there's still no tax to pay if you're a basic rate taxpayer but there could be some to pay if you're a higher rate taxpayer. Tax has already been paid by the life insurance company and can't be reclaimed by non-taxpayers. Complicated rules apply to taking income from 'non-qualifying plans' and to the potential tax bill of higher rate taxpayers – ask the company to explain, or see *Which?* Tax-Saving Guide (published annually in March).

Good for Anyone seeking a medium-risk investment. Regular premium plans are good for people who can commit themselves to regular saving for a long period. Single premium plans can be useful if you want a regular income.

Bad for People who really want life insurance. People who might need their money back early.

TIP *With-profits insurance policies provide a half-way house, in terms of risk, between the relatively safe but generally low-earning deposit-type investments and the relatively high-risk–high-return investments, such as shares, unit trusts and unit-linked life insurance.*

Shares and investment trusts

Where from Through a stockbroker or other share dealing service, through an investment adviser, or through new issues advertised in newspapers.

How they work You buy a stake in a company and become a part-owner of it along with all the other shareholders. The types of shares available range from shares in old-established companies to shares in very young companies, in different industries, even in different countries. You usually buy and sell in the hope of making a capital gain, though if share prices move against you, you could just as easily make a loss. Many shares also pay out regular dividends – usually twice a year – which give you an immediate share in the company's profits.

Investment trusts are companies which don't carry on a normal business themselves but instead buy and sell the shares of other companies and make other investments. By buying the shares of an investment trust you can buy into a ready-made portfolio of a range of different shares and investments. Unless you have a lot of money to invest, this will be a cheaper and more feasible way of spreading your money and your risk across a range of different shares and investments.

Minimum investment In theory none. In practice, dealing costs are disproportionately high on purchases or sales below, say, £1,500. You can invest smaller amounts at lower cost in the shares of some investment trusts using special savings schemes that they run.

Maximum investment None.

Tax Dividends count as taxable income and are paid with the equivalent of basic rate tax already deducted. You get tax credit as evidence of the tax already paid and non-taxpayers can use this to reclaim the tax. Basic rate taxpayers have no more tax to pay. Higher rate taxpayers pay extra tax.

Good for People who can afford to take a risk in the hope of a higher return – though consider also investment trusts or investments *linked* to shares as an alternative to direct investment.

Bad for Anyone who may need their money back at short notice – perhaps when share prices are low. Anyone who can't afford the risk that the value of their capital might fall.

WARNING
Always take into account the costs of dealing in shares when considering them as an investment. There will usually be a minimum commission – for example, £25 – regardless of the amount you are buying or selling; this makes small deals prohibitively expensive. Even if you invest a reasonable sum, you may need to see a rise in the price of your shares of, say, five per cent or more before you start to make any gain.

TIP
You can save on dealing costs by buying new issues of shares, such as the newly privatised issues. You can buy new shares directly without using a broker – you apply for a 'prospectus' which contains an application form or you can use an application form printed in a newspaper. But, though you incur no dealing costs when you buy a new issue, remember that you'll incur costs when you come to sell and that these could wipe out most or all of any gain.

WARNING
Be wary of claims made for 'penny shares'. Owning 10,000 shares which cost 1p each has no inherent advantage over owning 100 shares costing £1 each. Though both may cost the same, the return you get will depend on the quality of the company, and on average you'll do better with 100 shares in a solid household name than 1,000 shares in a high risk venture.

TIP
Consider a Personal Equity Plan (PEP) as a tax-efficient way of investing in shares. With these, income and gains from your investment are tax-free. Within limits, you can use PEPs to invest in investment trust shares or in unit trusts (see below) as long as the investment or unit trusts invest mainly in UK shares. You can include newly-issued shares that you buy after 6 April 1989 in your PEP. You can get details of PEPs from banks, unit trusts and building societies that run schemes, or from investment advisers.

Unit trusts

Where from Unit trust managers or through banks or investment advisers.

How they work Buying units in a unit trust is a relatively cheap way of spreading your money and risk across a range of shares and other investments. Instead of buying shares directly, you buy units in a fund of shares (and possibly other investments) which is run by professional fund managers. The value of your units rises and falls as the values of the underlying investments rise and fall. Your return is usually made up of two parts: income and capital gain (or loss). The income may be distributed to you at regular intervals or it may be automatically re-invested. Different unit trusts specialise in different areas of investment – for example, UK shares, British Government stocks, Japanese shares, smaller companies, and so on.

Minimum investment Varies – for example, £250 for a lump sum, or £25 a month for regular savings.

Maximum investment None.

Tax Income is taxable, even when it's automatically re-invested. Income has tax at the basic rate already deducted. You get a tax credit in a similar manner to income from shares and non-taxpayers can use this to reclaim the tax paid. Basic rate taxpayers have no more tax to pay. Higher rate taxpayers pay extra tax.

Good for People who can afford to take a higher risk in the hope of a higher return, but who don't have enough money to create their own share portfolio. People who want to invest abroad without the extra fuss and administration often involved in direct investment in foreign shares.

Bad for Anyone who might need their money back at short notice – perhaps when unit prices are low. Anyone who can't take the risk of losing their capital.

TIP *For basic rate taxpayers, unit trusts or investment trusts (see above) are usually a better way of investing in a ready-made portfolio than investing through unit-linked life insurance (see over).*

WARNING *Check what charges will be made. There are two main ways in which unit trust charges are generally made: the* 'bid-offer spread' *and an annual management charge.*

You buy units at the 'offer price' which is around 6 per cent higher than the 'bid price' at which you could sell the units – make sure you distinguish between the two prices when keeping track of your investment. Annual management charges vary at around 1½ to 2 per cent a year of the value of the investments in the trust.

TIP *Under the Financial Services Act, unit trusts can be sold on a 'cold calling' basis – in other words by salespeople on your doorstep (see p. 21). Be wary of buying in this way – you don't get a chance to look around properly and consider what's on the market. A 14 day 'cooling-off' period is allowed during which you can change your mind and cancel the deal, but you may still end up paying something. This is because the unit trust is allowed to recover from you a loss made if unit prices fall during the cooling-off period.*

TIP *There are different pricing systems in use in the unit trust industry and this can make a difference to the price you pay. Under 'historic' pricing, the price you pay has been calculated at the close of the previous day's business. With 'forward' pricing, the price is not calculated until after you've placed your order. And with 'real time' or 'frequent valuation' pricing, the unit price is recalculated throughout the day. Assuming other factors aren't more important to you, choose a trust that uses the pricing system which best suits you.*

Unit-linked life insurance

Where from Life insurance companies, life insurance brokers and other investment advisers.

How they work Depends on the type of plan. The structure of the plans is the same as for with-profits policies (see p. 129), but instead of earning bonuses, your money is used to buy units in one or more investment funds – rather like a unit trust (see above). The price of the units reflects the value of the underlying investments and can go down as well as up. Different funds specialise in different investment areas and you can usually switch part or all of your money from one fund to another (though there may be charges and restrictions on the amount moved or left in each fund).

Minimum investment Varies – for example around £20 a month for regular saving and £1,000 for a lump sum.

Maximum investment Usually none.

Tax Same as for with-profits policies (see p. 129).

Good for Regular savings plans are good for higher rate taxpayers who can commit themselves to regular saving. Single premium plans are good for higher rate taxpayers who've used up their capital gains tax allowance, and for people who want to switch investment area frequently while keeping a spread of investments.

Bad for Basic rate and non-taxpayers can usually do better with unit or investments trusts, as can anyone who has unused capital gains tax allowance. Regular savings plans are bad for anyone who can't commit themselves to regular saving.

WARNING *With all investments involving a managed fund – for example, unit trusts and unit-linked life insurance – check what charges will be made and how they'll be levied before you invest. And watch out with life insurance plans – there are often extra charges such as a policy fee, capital units bearing higher yearly charges, reduced unit allocations, and surrender penalties if you cash in early. At present, it's hard to make much sense of the list of various charges that apply to unit-linked life insurance. Under new rules proposed under the Financial Services Act, the overall impact of charges for unit-linked life insurance plans will, from January 1990 onwards, have to be shown as a proportion of the amount you're investing.*

WARNING *Life insurance plans also provide some life cover, but usually this is minimal with an investment-type life insurance such as the type described above. If you need life cover, it's an expensive way of getting adequate cover. Don't choose these plans, choose protection-only (term) insurance – it's much cheaper (see p. 104 for details) – and sort out your investment needs separately.*

7

Getting investment advice

It is not often that any man can have so much knowledge of another, as is necessary to make instruction useful. Samuel Johnson

Growing wealth and deliberate government policy are encouraging even small investors to take a more active approach to saving and investing, and to consider a wider range of investments. Even those who count their savings in hundreds rather than thousands are tempted by high-profile media campaigns to buy shares in privatisation issues, such as British Telecom and British Gas. More than 20 per cent of the population are now shareholders; 65 per cent of households have mortgages to help them buy their homes; 80 per cent of households have some sort of insurance policy, many of which are investment-type plans. The new legislation enabling employees to opt out of their company pension scheme and seek the best terms in the wider marketplace brings yet more people into the investment field.

There is a need for a greater awareness of personal financial planning. The wrong choice of investments can cost you thousands of pounds, not just in missed opportunities for a better return elsewhere, but possibly even losing your original savings if, say, a company collapses. So it is essential to understand something of the choices open to you and to pick the right person if you need financial advice.

Being your own investment adviser

To manage your own investment affairs successfully, whether they are simple or complex, can be hard work. You need to learn enough about tax, insurance, pensions and investments to enable you to work out your needs and then match them to appropriate financial products. You'll then need to keep abreast of changes which might affect your financial decisions. You'll need some good basic and unbiased books to cover the groundwork, and you should diligently read the personal finance columns in the press, follow the financial programmes on radio and television, and study the leaflets and documents issued by financial institutions to describe their products. You could perhaps subscribe to one or two specialist money magazines to help narrow down your choices from the vast range of products and companies available. Few people have enough time to tackle their finances properly, so a professional financial adviser could be the answer.

Getting the best from a financial adviser

Do your homework

Unfortunately, using an adviser doesn't absolve you from all the hard work – if you're to get the best from an adviser you need to have a clear idea of what your financial aims are:

- what sort of advice do you need? Perhaps a one-off assessment of your investment position, if, say, you've just come into a lump sum through inheritance, redundancy or retirement. Maybe you need regular investment advice, even someone to take over the management of your investments. Perhaps the problem is not so much your investment strategy overall, but how to manage the tax aspects, or maybe you're concerned about handing on your wealth when you die. Different types of adviser will best suit different aims
- what are your investment aims? Do you want income or capital growth? How much can you invest – on a regular basis, or as a lump sum? How long can you invest for? How much risk do you want to take?

Ideally, you should also find out something about basic financial planning and the main types of investment available (see Chapter 6). The more knowledge you acquire *before* going to an adviser, the more fruitful your discussion is likely to be.

Contact two or three advisers

There are many sources of investment advice – general advisers, insurance advisers, stockbrokers, banks, building societies, solicitors, accountants, or going to investment providers direct. On pp. 145–51, you'll find details of each to help you find the right type of adviser.

Draw up a shortlist of two or three advisers and talk to them all before settling on one. Compare the questions they ask you as well as the answers they give to your questions, and avoid advisers who don't ask enough questions. Any adviser should find out enough about your financial situation and aims so that they can identify the right investments for you. The Financial Services Act 1986 reinforces this duty, and specifically requires investment advisers to 'know their customers'. Many advisers will ask you to complete a special form as a basic checklist of your circumstances and requirements.

TIP *As a minimum, an adviser will need information about all the following areas in order to give you sound advice: your age and health, whether you're married, single, separated or divorced, the number and ages of any children and any other dependants, the size and make-up of the family's income, possible changes in your financial circumstances, your regular financial commitments, your tax position, your home and mortgage, your existing insurance, pension arrangements and investments, if any, your investment aims, how much you have to invest, how much access you want to your money, and what risk you can take.*

Check the advisers' credentials

Although most people in the financial services business are honest and competent the Financial Services Act 1986 was designed to shut the door on the minority which fall into neither category. Under the Act, it is a criminal offence for any investment business (whether it's a provider of investments or a giver of advice) to operate without authorisation. An investment business must be authorised by a Self Regulating Organisation (SRO) or by the overall regulating body – the Securities and Investments Board (SIB). There are five SROs:

- the Financial Intermediaries, Managers and Brokers Regulatory Association (FIMBRA) covers investment intermediaries who advise on or manage investments for individuals
- the Life Assurance and Unit Trust Regulatory Organisation (LAUTRO) covers insurance companies, unit trusts and friendly societies and is concerned mainly with the selling and marketing of their products
- The Securities Association (TSA) is made up of members of the Stock Exchange plus dealers in some other stocks, bonds and so on
- the Investment Management Regulatory Organisation (IMRO) consists of corporate fund managers and advisers, such as pension fund managers and unit trust managers, plus some banks
- the Association of Futures Brokers and Dealers (AFBD) is made up of investment businesses involved with futures and options.

Members of certain professions, such as solicitors and accountants, which give investment advice as a side line to their main business can be authorised by a Recognised Professional Body (RPB). But if their investment business is substantial, they will have to be authorised through an SRO. There's a list of SROs and RPBs together with their addresses and phone numbers on pp. 156–8.

CASE HISTORY

Miss G filled in a form to enter a prize draw competition. She wasn't surprised that she didn't win but she was surprised to receive a series of phone calls from a company who tried to persuade her to invest in the futures market. Futures contracts are a way of gambling on the price of certain commodites. They are highly risky and are suitable only for investors who can afford to lose money. Only the most irresponsible investment adviser would suggest that a private investor of limited means like Miss G should consider them. Yet she was plagued by phone calls telling her that she could double her money in a fortnight. She weakened and sent a cheque for well over £1,500.

A couple of days later the company rang her again, informing her that her investment had nearly doubled – but they advised her against taking her profit 'as the time wasn't right'. The salesman rang again the next day, saying that her investment had gone down to less than its original value. Miss G decided to cut her losses before things got worse, but she was told that her money had already been reinvested. She was told to send more money but wisely refused. The following day the salesman rang a third time and said that the original investment was now worth less than a third of its original value and too derisory an amount to re-invest, so he sent her that amount back.

When the SIB receive complaints about such high-pressure sales techniques – charging such high commission that clients are unlikely to make a profit, and ignoring clients' instructions – they can suspend the company from trading and apply for it to be wound up as 'not fit to carry on the business of broking in futures and options'.

For a business to be authorised it must be 'fit and proper' and must meet various solvency requirements. It must carry out its business according to the rules of its SRO, RPB or the SIB. If a business breaks the rules, it will be subject to various disciplinary procedures and, if the breach is serious, it could have its authorisation taken away and be compulsorily wound up. If you lose money through an investment business's fraud or negligence, and the firm has gone into liquidation, you may be covered (at least to some extent) by the compensation scheme set up under the Act – see p. 165 for details.

You can check whether or not an investment business is authorised, and by which SRO or RPB, by consulting a register, kept and updated by the SIB, either through Prestel (available in most main libraries) or by phoning 01-929 3652. An investment business must also make clear on its stationery by which SRO or RPB it is authorised.

Independent advice or not?

An important point to consider before making your choice is whether you are happy to consider the products of just one company, or whether you want independent advice about the full range of products available. Under the Financial Services Act, all investment advisers must give advice on one of those two bases. For example, a few banks and the odd building society offer independent advice through their branch network. Most other banks and building societies have decided to tie themselves to a single insurance company for the purpose of selling life insurance and pensions through their branches, though they may also run a totally separate subsidiary offering independent advice. Many general and insurance advisers are tied to a single insurance company, others are independent. All solicitors and accountants giving investment advice are independent.

An adviser must make quite clear at the time you start to do business with him whether he is representing one company and, if so, which one, or whether he can give independent advice. If you're unsure of his status, ask him to clarify it. You can also check his status by consulting the SIB register (see above).

A group of insurance companies which seek new business through independent advisers set up the Campaign for Independent Financial Advice (CAMIFA) at the start of 1987 to promote awareness and use of independent advisers. A separate company, IFA (Promotions) Ltd, has now taken its place; you can phone them on 01-200 3000 for a list of ten independent advisers in your neighbourhood. Independent advisers are allowed to display a distinctive blue and white 'Independent Financial Adviser' logo at their premises and on stationery. Don't confuse this logo with information about the Self Regulating Organisation to which the adviser belongs.

'Best advice'

Under the Financial Services Act, advisers are obliged to give 'best advice' – though precisely what this means in practice is the subject of some debate. Broadly, independent advisers must monitor all the products on the market and regularly review them so that they can recommend to you a specific company's product which seems best suited to your needs. A 'tied' adviser can consider only the range of products of the company they represent and recommend the most suitable from those – if none is suitable, the adviser should tell you.

TIP *Don't assume your adviser is giving bad advice just because they don't recommend the investments or companies at the top of the performance leagues. Past performance is no guide to the future; and a good adviser should be taking account of a whole range of factors, such as measures and indications of the financial soundness of the companies, the aims and level of risk inherent in their different investment strategies, the level of expenses and charges, and so on.*

WARNING *The SIB has interpreted rules under the Financial Services Act so that 'best advice' will allow independent advisers to recommend the product of just one company to a group of similar investors – for example, all customers seeking low-cost endowment mortgages might be recommended just one insurance company's policy. The product to be recommended must be reviewed from time to time, and a new company's product chosen if this would be better. In the absence of this interpretation, you would probably have been offered a short list of two or three different companies. Don't accept the recommended product if you're not happy with it – go to another adviser who's willing to give you a choice.*

Check the cost of advice

Check how the adviser is to be paid. Some charge fees, which might be based on how much time the adviser spends on your case, or on the amount of money you have to invest. Stockbrokers will charge you commission on the value of the shares you are buying or selling. An insurance company representative can be paid in some or all of the following ways – salary, fringe benefits, commissions, bonuses. But the vast majority of independent advisers are paid largely through commissions from the companies whose products they sell – though some, including solicitors and accountants, are paid wholly or partly through fees that they charge.

Don't assume advice is free just because you pay nothing directly. The cost of paying commissions to advisers – whether independent or tied – is taken into account in setting the level of charges for a product, and is a major reason for the hefty surrender penalties if you cash in a life insurance product early. An adviser earns different levels of commission for selling different types of product. Selling some products – such as National Savings investments – earns no commission at all.

If you ask, an independent (but not a tied) adviser must tell you how much commission they'll receive from selling you a particular product. At present, if you don't ask, you won't get any direct information about commissions at the time you buy a product. An independent adviser might be paid in accordance with an old scale of commissions called the Maximum Commission Agreement (MCA) – if so, you'll be told this, and you can get details of the MCA from LAUTRO. More likely, the adviser will be paid more than the MCA rates – you'll be told that this is the case, but you won't get details of the amount of commission that the adviser is getting until you receive the full product details up to 14 days after you've bought the product. It's proposed that from January 1990 you'll only be given information about commission up to 14 days after you've bought the product. The details must usually include a 'cancellation notice' which tells you that you have a period of 14 days from receiving the notice within which you can change your mind about the deal. But having got so far, it's unlikely that you'd cancel the deal just because the amount of commission being paid to the adviser looked too high. The SIB plans to publish regular surveys of the levels of commission being paid to independent advisers, so that you can have an idea of the appropriate level for the product you're interested in.

WARNING *Under the Financial Services Act, an adviser should act in your interests and give you best advice (see opposite) regardless of how much or how little commission they stand to earn. Nevertheless, it's a good idea to ask the adviser how much commission they'll get on the various investments that might suit you, and to check again the reasons for any recommendation if you think commission* *might be influencing the adviser. If you're still unhappy about the recommendation, don't take it up and consult another adviser.*

TIP *Seemingly free advice is not necessarily the cheapest or best. Paying a direct fee to an adviser could work out cheaper in the long run.*

Get everything in writing

An adviser must usually ask you to sign a 'client agreement' setting out the terms of the contract between you. Unfortunately, this requirement doesn't apply where the adviser is selling you just life insurance, unit trusts or pensions. The salient points of the agreement may be set out in terms of a business letter, but if they are not, or if there are additional points which you think should be noted, keep your own record of what was discussed and agreed.

Whether or not there's a client agreement, it's a good idea to keep a note of the time, date, person you spoke to, and content of any telephone conversations and meetings. Confirm in writing if possible (keeping a copy for yourself). These notes could be vital if you have a dispute with the adviser.

Be careful with cheques

Once upon a time, the unscrupulous adviser could happily mix clients' money with his own, often making it impossible to untangle who owned what if the adviser went bust. Under the Financial Services Act, advisers who are allowed to accept client money (many are not) must keep it in a separate client account – though this can be one account for all clients, not one for each, so ownership could still be disputed.

But unless the adviser is taking investment decisions for you (as with a 'discretionary management' service), there's usually no need for you to hand money to him at all. Instead, make cheques payable to the company providing the investment – be insistent, if necessary. This may seem inconvenient if you are investing in several different companies at one time, as you'll need to make out several cheques, but doing so will reduce the likelihood of a fraudulent adviser diverting your funds into his own pocket.

Which adviser?

The following pages give a run down of the main types of financial advisers and what they have to offer. For details of what protection and rights of action you have if things go wrong, see Chapter 8.

General investment advisers

Who they are They go under a variety of names – for example, personal investment adviser, investment manager, collective investment intermediary, investment dealer, investment broker. They should be prepared to give advice about the full range of available investments but some may turn out to be just insurance advisers.

What they offer General investment advice on, for example, pensions, unit trusts, life insurance policies, shares, advice on tax, their own investment management services.

What they charge Varies. With life insurance or unit trusts you pay nothing to the adviser because he gets commission from the company whose product he sells to you. If you ask him to take on lump sum management on your behalf, the charge will be on a percentage basis – say, a half to one per cent of the value of your portfolio, charged on a yearly basis (sometimes, less for larger amounts). Or there might be a flat fee, or a slice of the profits.

Who they are authorised by Usually FIMBRA, IMRO or TSA.

TIP *Some advisers have more expertise in one area than another – ask whether they specialise before you do business.*

Insurance advisers

Who they are These may be company representatives or independent advisers. Anyone can use the title 'adviser' or 'consultant' but 'brokers' must be registered with the Insurance Brokers' Registration Council (IBRC) – this lays down its own rules regarding conduct of business. Brokers must give independent advice.

What they offer Advice on insurance and pensions. Some also offer tax advice, unit trust advice, and an investment management service. Some insurance brokers advise on and arrange general insurance, such as car insurance, holiday and household insurance (see Chapter 5).

What they charge Usually nothing – they get commission from the companies whose products they sell. For investment management services, charges will be similar to those for general advisers (see p. 145).

Who they are authorised by Usually FIMBRA, though brokers who do a limited amount of investment business might be authorised by virtue of their membership of the IBRC (a Recognised Professional Body). Company representatives will be covered by LAUTRO.

TIP *Although no authorised adviser is supposed to take into consideration their commission when recommending a policy, you could ask about life policies from the few insurance companies who don't pay commission (such as Equitable Life and Ecclesiastical), if none have been mentioned. The adviser might charge you a fee if they arrange a policy with a non-commission company.*

Stockbrokers

Who they are Members of The International Stock Exchange of the United Kingdom and Republic of Ireland, and bound by that body's rules to ensure fair dealing.

What they offer Advice on buying and selling shares and British Government stocks. Advice on buying and selling some other more specialist investments, such as traded options and corporate bonds. Some also offer advice about unit trusts, their own unit trust and Personal Equity Plan schemes, investment research, and general investment advice.

What they charge Commission when they buy and sell on your behalf – usually between one and two per cent of the price paid plus VAT with a minimum commission that might be around £25, say. Some brokers offer a cheaper 'dealing only' ('execution only') service which means they'll carry out your buying and selling instructions but give no advice. For investment management, there will be a fee of, say, one per cent a year of the value of your investments.

Who they are authorised by TSA.

TIP *Traditional stockbroking services are often expensive, especially if you buy and sell relatively small amounts of shares, but charges vary a lot, so shop around. The big banks and some building societies offer stockbroking services which may work out cheaper.*

Solicitors

Who they are They are not generally investment specialists but many either offer investment services as an adjunct to their normal business or can refer you to an investment specialist. All solicitors who offer such services give independent advice.

What they offer Varies – for example, advice on ways of passing money on, tax planning, advice on general investment strategy, sometimes an investment management service, links with specialists such as stock-brokers. They might also be able to help with mortgages, and some general insurance such as house buildings insurance, as a corollary to a conveyancing service. The Law Societies have arranged a special financial advice service (appropriately authorised under the Financial Services Act) which solicitors can join and use to obtain advice for their clients.

What they charge Usually a fee which will depend on the time spent on your case. If they arrange life insurance, unit trusts or share purchases for you, they'll usually get commission. They must pass this on to you and, in practice, this will usually be done by offsetting commissions against the fees you would otherwise pay – unless you specifically agree that the solicitor may keep all or part of the commission. But if the solicitor uses the financial advice service set up by the Law Society, part of any commission is paid to the advice service.

Who they are authorised by Usually by their professional bodies – the Law Society of England and Wales, the Law Society of Scotland, or the Law Society of Northern Ireland – which are Recognised Professional Bodies. Solicitors with substantial investment business may belong to FIMBRA.

Note In most cases, solicitors must be authorised by an SRO if more than 20 to 25 per cent of their work comes from investment advice. But the Law Society of Scotland has defined the limit as the maximum allowed under SIB rules, which is 49.9 per cent.

TIP *Check that a solicitor has the particular expertise that you need before asking them to handle your investment business. They may use the financial advice service set up by the Law Society (see above).*

Accountants

Who they are Not investment specialists, but they may offer investment advice as an adjunct to their main business, or might refer you to an investment specialist. All accountants must give independent advice.

What they offer Varies – for example, tax planning, advice on general investment strategy, sometimes investment management services, and contacts with specialists such as stockbrokers. Large firms, in particular, may offer a very comprehensive range of investment services through specialist in-house departments.

What they charge Usually their normal fees which are based on the time spent on your case. If they arrange insurance, unit trusts or share purchase for you, they may receive commission. They must tell you about any commissions they receive and in practice will often set off at least part of any commissions against the fees charged.

Who they are authorised by Through membership of one of their professional bodies – the Chartered Association of Certified Accountants, Institute of Chartered Accountants in England and Wales, Institute of Chartered Accountants of Scotland, or Institute of Chartered Accountants in Ireland, which are Recognised Professional Bodies. Accountants with substantial investment business may also belong to FIMBRA.

TIP *Check that the accounting firm you go to has the particular specialist knowledge you need before asking them to handle your investment business.*

Banks

Who they are All the major High Street banks offer investment advice, either through their branch network, or through connected companies.

Some offer independent advice, some are tied to a particular company for the purpose of selling life insurance and pensions. Others manage to offer both types of advice by having a 'tied' branch network but an independent subsidiary which operates at arm's length from the branches.

What they offer Varies. This could include advice on the bank's own products, such as a wide range of deposit/savings accounts, life insurance, unit trusts, pensions, and Personal Equity Plans. Might offer independent advice, dealing service for, and maybe advice on, buying and selling shares, advice on tax and pensions, investment management service.

What they charge Usually nothing if you buy life insurance, pensions or unit trusts as the bank gets commission. Usually, normal stockbroking commissions for share dealing (see p. 146), though rates and/or minimum commissions may be a bit lower than with traditional broking services. Either a flat fee or a half to one per cent a year of the value of your investments with an investment management service. There may be an extra charge for tax advice and help.

Who they are authorised by Depends which bank service you're dealing with. An insurance or unit trust arm will be authorised by LAUTRO and probably IMRO as well. An independent advice arm will usually be authorised through FIMBRA, and stockbroking services will require the bank to belong to TSA. Note that other bank services such as mortgages (other than related endowment insurance), personal banking, loans and deposit-type investments are outside the scope of the Financial Services Act.

WARNING *Always check the status of the particular bit of the bank or building society that you're dealing with. Some offer an independent investment advice service. But most banks and building societies now offer a 'tied' service through their branch networks. There may be a separate arm of the business which gives independent advice, but unless you have a lot to invest, you might not be steered towards the independent arm unless you make a point of asking about it.*

Building societies

What they are Many building societies have decided to take advantage of the freedom given them under the Building Societies Act 1986 to offer a much more extensive range of services than the ones they traditionally specialised in. They are still mainly providers of mortgages and deposit-type savings accounts. But their other activities also include selling and recommending life insurance and pensions – either the products of one company or on an independent basis.

What they offer Advice in connection with mortgages, including related life insurance and pensions, more general advice on, for example, life insurance and unit trusts, advice on their own products – for example, a wide range of deposit-type savings schemes and certain pension products. Some also offer share dealing as agent for a stockbroker.

What they charge Usually nothing because the society gets commission from the company whose products it sells. If the society passes you on to another adviser – for example, a stockbroker – you pay that adviser's fees.

Who they are authorised by Usually the SIB. Note that activities such as mortgages (except for related life insurance and pensions), other loans, personal banking, and deposit-type savings schemes are outside the scope of the Financial Services Act.

Going direct to a company

Who they are Many life insurance and unit trust companies are happy to deal with you direct, though if you do this some companies will pass your name on to an adviser for you to deal through.

What they offer Obviously, they will try to sell you their own products, so you should deal direct with a company only if you know exactly what you want or are happy to invest in just that company's products. Their services may include advice about the relative merits of their products and whether they are suitable for you, general information about financial markets, retirement planning services, investment management within their own range of unit trusts, say.

What they charge   Whatever charges are built into the products (which you'd also pay using an adviser). Usually a flat fee or, say, a quarter to a half of one per cent for a unit trust management service.

WARNING *The cost of paying commission to independent advisers is built into the charging structure for a company's products. You pay the same charges whether you use an adviser or go to the company direct.*

Who they are authorised by   LAUTRO and IMRO.

TIP *Unless you have a special reason for going to a particular company, get advice and quotes from several before making a choice.*

8

Investment complaints

The virtue of prosperity is temperance; the virtue of adversity is fortitude. Francis Bacon

The UK now has a fairly rigorous system to protect investors against losing money through bad management or unscrupulous dealing by an investment provider or adviser. But no system can totally protect you: some incompetents may slip through, the really determined fraudster can find ways around the rules, and sometimes perfectly genuine mistakes happen. So there is always the possibility that the investment products that you buy, or the service that you get, will be in some way faulty. For example, you might suspect that you were given less than sound investment advice, you might not be getting the documents or regular investment reviews that you think you should have, or in the worst event the firm to which you entrusted your savings might go bust.

WARNING *No investor protection system is designed to protect you from the risks inherent in the investments themselves. It should ensure that you are adequately informed of the risks and not deliberately or negligently advised to take an unsuitable course of action. But ultimately, if you choose to invest in, say, shares, you must accept the risk that the amount of your investment might fall rather than rise, and not expect compensation if losses result.*

What can you do if you think you have a legitimate grievance against an investment company or adviser? In most cases, there are formal steps that you can take to try to get your problem resolved, and in the last resort you may be covered by a compensation scheme. But before invoking a formal complaints procedure, you should take up the matter with the company concerned.

TIP *Complaints procedures, particularly once you've exhausted those of the company concerned, can seem complicated and even daunting. But you should be signposted, at each stage, to the steps you can take next – you don't need a grasp of the whole system at once.*

Complain to the company

First discuss your complaint with the person you initially dealt with, whether it's the broker who bought shares for you, the person who sold you an insurance policy, or the counter staff in the building society who arranged to open your share account. If the matter is a simple one it might well be resolved on the spot.

If an immediate solution is not possible but further checking or investigation is required, give the person a chance, and the time they ask for, to investigate. But make clear that you'll expect to hear from them within a specified time, or that you'll be in touch again after a specified time.

If no satisfactory action or explanation results from your initial approaches, gather together all the facts relating to your complaint (including the names of people you've spoken to and when the conversations occurred) and any evidence you have to back it up, and write to the senior person at the firm or branch you're dealing with – this will usually be the manager; if you're not sure who to address your letter to phone up and ask for the name of an appropriate person.

If the manager's response isn't satisfactory, you'll have to take the complaint higher. If you've been dealing with a branch or subsidiary, you should pass your complaint to the firm's head office. The address will almost certainly be printed on any leaflets the firm produces, and may be on any letters you've had from them. Address your letter to the Complaints Department or, if you know that the company comes within the scope of the Financial Services Act, you could address it to the Compliance Officer (who is responsible for seeing that the company operates within the rules of the Act). If you're unsure who to address it to, phone the head office and ask for the name of an appropriate contact. Most libraries keep a directory which will give you the name of the chief executive, managing director or chairman, as well as the address of the company's head office, so write to them if you have no other contact.

TIP *Whenever you complain to someone who was not directly involved in the business under dispute, do so in writing rather than orally. It's helpful to include a brief summary of events giving relevant dates and the names of people you've been dealing with. Don't forget to include any reference or account numbers. It's useful to enclose relevant letters and documents but make sure you send only copies, and keep the originals yourself.*

If you've exhausted the company's complaints system and still had no satisfaction, you'll have to step outside the company to seek help. Who you turn to depends on the type of organisation and the type of product or service involved.

Complaints covered by the Financial Services Act

All investment businesses covered by the Act must have an internal complaints system. If that is insufficient to resolve a dispute, there are several other levels through which you can take your complaint. In addition to the complaints procedures under the Act, there are other bodies who can deal with complaints, and these are dealt with later in the chapter.

What the Act covers

The Financial Services Act applies to all organisations 'carrying on investment business in the UK'. 'Investment' as defined in the Act doesn't include a few things that you'd normally think of as investments, such as bank and building society deposit savings accounts, deposit-based pensions, or National Savings Bank accounts. But it covers the majority of investment products and services.

WARNING *If you're dealing with a business permanently based in the UK, the Financial Services Act will apply. If you're dealing with a business based overseas, the Act won't cover you in many cases. This means that there may be no safeguards to ensure that the firm is honest and competent, and no compensation if things do go wrong. Some overseas countries have their own investor protection rules that might apply, but these are usually not as rigorous as the UK rules, and often there is no protection at all. So you should check an overseas company's credentials very carefully before risking your money with it, and if you have any doubts, don't invest.*

The regulators

The Financial Services Act itself just sets out a framework of rules. The real regulation is in the hands of the Securities and Investments Board (SIB), which has delegated many of its day-to-day powers to the five Self Regulating Organisations (SROs). All investment businesses must be 'authorised' either directly by the SIB or by belonging to one of the SROs, and they must abide by the rules of the regulating body.

Some professions (such as solicitors and accountants), which conduct investment business which is 'incidental' to their main activities, need not belong to an SRO, but can be authorised by a professional body which has been granted the status of a Recognised Professional Body (RPB).

If you have a complaint which hasn't been dealt with satisfactorily by the company concerned, you may be able to take it to an Ombudsman or Referee scheme (see p. 158). Alternatively, you could take it to the relevant SRO, RPB, or the SIB (if the business is authorised directly by the SIB). If you're not happy with the way an SRO or RPB handles your case, you can refer it to the SIB itself. If the SRO, RPB or the SIB thinks that rules have been broken, they will investigate the company and may

take disciplinary action against it. Your case may be referred to a special complaints procedure, such as the relevant Ombudsman or Referee scheme. The SIB, the SROs and the RPBs all have slightly different complaints procedures, but all have such a mechanism. And all will refer your case on to the appropriate body, if you initially approach the wrong one, or if findings suggest that one of the other bodies should be involved.

An investment business must make clear to customers which SRO, or RPB (or the SIB) it belongs to – for example, this information must be included on any business cards or stationery. Also, you can find out by consulting the SIB register (see p. 141).

The names, addresses and phone numbers of the SIB, the SROs and RPBs are given below:

Securities and Investments Board (SIB)
3 Royal Exchange Buildings, London EC3V 3NL
Tel: 01-283 2474
(Direct members include some building societies)

Self Regulating Organisations (SROs)

Association of Futures Brokers and Dealers (AFBD)
B Section, 5th Floor, Plantation House, 5–8 Mincing Lane, London EC3M 3DX
Tel: 01-626 9763
(Members are advisers, managers and dealers in futures and options)

Financial Intermediaries, Managers and Brokers Regulatory Association (FIMBRA)
Hertsmere House, Marsh Wall, London E14 9RW
Tel: 01-538 8860
(Members are independent investment advisers and managers)

Investment Management Regulatory Organisation (IMRO)
Centre Point, 103 New Oxford Street, London WC1A 1PT
Tel: 01-379 0601
(Members are institutional investment advisers, investment and pension fund managers, and trustees. Banks may be members in respect of relevant parts of their business)

Life Assurance and Unit Trust Regulatory Organisation (LAUTRO)
Centre Point, 103 New Oxford Street, London WC1A 1QH
Tel: 01-379 0444
(Members are life insurance companies, unit trusts and friendly societies)

The Securities Association (TSA)
The Stock Exchange Tower, London EC2N 1HP
Tel: 01-256 9000
(Made up of members of the Stock Exchange plus dealers in some other marketable investments)

Recognised Professional Bodies (RPBS)

Chartered Association of Certified Accountants
29 Lincoln's Inn Fields, London WC2A 3EE
Tel: 01-242 6855

Institute of Actuaries
Staple Inn Hall, High Holborn, London WC1V 7QJ
Tel: 01-242 0106

Institute of Chartered Accountants in England and Wales
PO Box 433, Chartered Accountants' Hall, Moorgate Place, London EC2P 2BJ
Tel: 01-628 7060

Institute of Chartered Accountants in Ireland
Chartered Accountants House, 87/89 Pembroke Road, Dublin 4
Tel: 0001 680400

Institute of Chartered Accountants of Scotland
27 Queen Street, Edinburgh EH2 1LA
Tel: 031-255 5673

Insurance Brokers Registration Council (IBRC)
15 St Helen's Place, London EC3A 6DS
Tel: 01-588 4387

The Law Society
113 Chancery Lane, London WC2A 1PL
Tel: 01-242 1222

Law Society of Northern Ireland
Law Society House, 90–106 Victoria Street, Belfast BT1 3JZ
Tel: 0232 231614

Law Society of Scotland
Law Society's Hall, 26 Drumsheugh Gardens, Edinburgh EH3 7YR
Tel: 031-226 7411

Ombudsman and Referee schemes

Most of the SROs have special schemes for dealing with complaints from the public. These provide a readily accessible route for settling disputes by using an independent arbitrator to consider the evidence on both sides and decide or recommend an equable solution. The schemes fall into two types: Ombudsman schemes under which you are not bound by any decision and can take your complaint still further by turning to the courts; and Referee schemes under which you're bound by the decision reached and give up your right to go to court. Your complaint may be referred to the scheme by the SRO, or you can contact them direct. Brief details of the schemes most relevant to private investors are given in the following sections.

WARNING *You must usually have exhausted the internal complaints procedure of the investment firm you're dealing with before the Ombudsman or Referee schemes can take up your case.*

The Insurance Ombudsman Bureau

What it is Scheme set up in 1981 to deal with a wide range of insurance complaints (including general insurance, such as car and house insurance), and which is now, for investment-type life insurance, part of the LAUTRO complaints mechanism. It's a voluntary scheme – most but not all insurance companies are members. The Bureau can't deal with complaints concerning companies who aren't members – LAUTRO would deal with these direct.

When you can complain Regarding any aspect of your dealings with a life insurance company except those areas specifically excluded (see opposite). Complaints might concern, say, dubious selling practices, or excessive delays in a company's dealings with you. The most common type of complaint concerns the failure of an insurer to pay a claim because of a dispute about what the policy actually says or means.

When you can't complain The main types of complaints that the Ombudsman can't deal with concern the calculation of bonuses, surrender values or overall returns on a life policy, and disputes about insurance intermediaries, such as brokers. The Ombudsman can only deal with disputes between you and your own insurer; he can't deal with 'third party' disputes – in other words, those involving claims against someone else's insurer.

Points to note You must take your case to the Ombudsman within six months of receiving a final offer from the company concerned. The Ombudsman's decision is binding on the company but not on you, so you can still take court action. He has the power to make awards up to £100,000 (or £10,000 a year, in cases about permanent health insurance). Contact:

Insurance Ombudsman Bureau
31 Southampton Row, London WC1B 5HJ
Tel: 01-242 8613

The Unit Trust Ombudsman
What it is Fairly new scheme started in October 1988 to look at complaints concerning unit trusts as part of the LAUTRO complaints mechanism. Voluntary scheme – not all unit trust companies are members, though it's hoped the number will rise as the scheme matures. The Ombudsman can't consider cases concerning companies which don't belong. But unit trust companies which belong to both IMRO and LAUTRO must in any case submit to the Investment Referee scheme (see p. 160), if they don't belong to the Unit Trust Ombudsman scheme.

When you can complain Concerning any aspect of your dealings with a unit trust company – for example, failure to carry out your instructions in good time, misleading advertisements and dubious selling practices.

When you can't complain The main type of complaint the Ombudsman can't deal with is insurance-linked units, but the Insurance Ombudsman deals with these.

INVESTMENT COMPLAINTS

Points to note You must take your complaint to the Ombudsman within six months of your last dealings with the company concerning the complaint. The Ombudsman's decision is binding on the company but not you. He has the power to make awards up to £100,000. Contact:

Unit Trust Ombudsman
31 Southampton Row, London WC1B 5HJ
Tel: 01-242 8613

The Investment Referee

What it is Scheme set up in early 1989 and used jointly by IMRO and FIMBRA to consider complaints about either IMRO members, or independent investment advisers and managers under the aegis of FIMBRA. All IMRO and FIMBRA members are covered by the scheme (though where an IMRO member also belongs to an Ombudsman scheme, your case may be referred to the Ombudsman Bureau).

When you can complain About virtually any loss of money which you think is due to the actions of an IMRO or FIMBRA member, or their failure to act, or due to their fault in some other way.

When you can't complain If more than 18 months have passed since you knew about the problem (or should have done). In the case of IMRO, if the event giving rise to the problem occurred before 30 April 1988. In the case of FIMBRA, if the event occurred before 1 April 1989.

Points to note The Referee will first try to settle the dispute through conciliation. If that doesn't work, you can take your case to court. Alternatively, if the Referee offers, you can agree to him acting as adjudicator, in which case, you give up your right to court action. The Referee will decide the case and the decision will be binding on both you and the company. The Referee has the power to make binding awards up to £50,000 in cases concerning FIMBRA members and £100,000 in cases concerning IMRA members. Contact:

Office of the Investment Referee
Centre Point, 103 New Oxford Street, London WC1A 1PT
Tel: 01-379 0601

WARNING *Many FIMBRA members are relatively small firms. Concern has been expressed that if the Referee were to order a firm to pay you up to £50,000, the firm might be unable to comply with the award due to insufficient funds. This could force the firm into liquidation, but, if there were still not enough funds to meet the award, you would have a claim against the SIB compensation scheme (see p. 165) which could pay you up to £48,000.*

TSA Complaints Bureau and Consumer Arbitration Scheme

What they are New schemes to deal with complaints concerning members of The Securities Association, such as stockbrokers. All members of TSA are covered by the schemes. The Complaints Bureau will investigate your complaint and try to conciliate between you and the broker (free of charge). If the Bureau can't resolve the dispute, you can take it to the Consumer Arbitration Scheme. This is for disputes involving sums up to £25,000; there is an initial fee of £10 but you may need legal help which will cost extra and, if your complaint is considered 'scandalous, frivolous, or vexatious', you may have to pay up to £500. There is also a more expensive Full Arbitration Scheme for disputes involving larger amounts.

When you can complain Concerning any aspect of your dealings with a stockbroker, such as failure to carry out your buying and selling instructions in good time, unacceptable delays in providing paperwork or sales proceeds and so on.

When you can't complain Where the event giving rise to the problem occurred before 29 April 1988.

Points to note You have up to two years in which to refer your complaint to the schemes. Any decision by the Complaints Bureau is not binding and you can take court action if you choose. Decisions of the arbitrator *are* binding and, in using the scheme, you give up your right to go to court. The Consumer Arbitration Scheme can make awards up to £25,000. Awards under the Full Arbitration Scheme are unlimited. Contact:

Complaints Bureau
TSA, The Stock Exchange Building, London EC2N 1EQ
Tel: 01-256 9000

SIB complaints procedure

What it is System for handling complaints against firms authorised directly by the SIB or against the SRO or RPB to which you took your complaint initially.

When you can complain About any aspect of your dealings with the firm. About any aspect of the way the SRO or RPB handled your complaint – but the SIB can't re-examine the original complaint itself.

When you can't complain When your complaint is against a company authorised by one of the SROs or RPBs (the SIB would pass your complaint to the relevant body). Similarly, if the company concerned belongs to one of the Ombudsman schemes, the SIB would refer the complaint to that scheme. If the event giving rise to the problem arose before 29 April 1988.

Points to note Initially, the SIB will try to conciliate between you and the company. If this is unsuccessful, your complaint may be referred to a panel of independent investigators. The panel will make recommendations or representations and, if these are unsuccessful, you could take the case to court. Alternatively, you could agree to arbitration, in which case, you give up your right to go to court. The decision of the arbitrator is binding on both you and the company. There is no limit on the amount of the claim. Contact:

Securities and Investments Board (SIB)
3 Royal Exchange Buildings, London EC3V 3NL
Tel: 01-283 2474

Complaints concerning banks

If your complaint is covered by the Financial Services Act – for example, it concerns the bank's insurance or unit trust products – the bank will be a member of an SRO and you should use the complaints procedures outlined in the previous section. But if it concerns the bank's products or activities falling outside the scope of the Act – for example, the bank's deposit-type savings accounts, its personal banking or mortgage services – you can (once you've exhausted the bank's internal complaints procedures) turn to the Banking Ombudsman for help.

TIP *For the purposes of the special complaints procedures described below, 'bank' includes Access and Barclaycard and a number of separate companies associated with the banks which belong to the Ombudsman scheme.*

The Office of the Banking Ombudsman

What it is Scheme started in 1986 to provide a low cost route for dealing with consumer complaints. Voluntary scheme – not all banks belong, though all the High Street banks do. The Ombudsman can't deal with complaints concerning banks who are not members.

When you can complain About most aspects of the bank's activities except those covered by the Financial Services Act. Typical complaints include disputes about cash machine withdrawals, bank charges, and the handling of accounts.

When you can't complain Some areas are excluded – for example, the level of the bank's general interest rate, and any disputes involving more than £100,000.

Points to note You must contact the Ombudsman within six months of your last dealings with the bank regarding the complaint, and the case must have arisen after 1 January 1986. The Ombudsman's decision is binding on the bank, but not you, so you can reject his decision and take your complaint to court if you wish. The Ombudsman has the power to make awards up to £100,000. Contact:

Office of the Banking Ombudsman
Citadel House, 5–11 Fetter Lane, London EC4A 1BR
Tel: 01-583 1395

Complaints concerning building societies

If your complaint falls within the scope of the Financial Services Act, the building society will be a member of the appropriate SRO or SIB and you should use the complaints procedures already described. If it's not covered by the Act, and you've exhausted the society's internal complaints procedure, you could take your case to the Building Societies Ombudsman.

The Office of the Building Societies Ombudsman

What it is Scheme started in 1987 to provide a low cost route for dealing with consumer complaints. It's a statutory scheme (under the Building Societies Act 1986). All societies are members.

When you can complain About most aspects of building society products and services, except those arising before the mortgage or investment was completed. The biggest area of work is, not surprisingly, mortgages. Other typical complaints concern investment accounts and disputed cash machine withdrawals.

When you can't complain Excluded areas include, at present, some of the new areas that building societies have moved into, such as deposit-based personal pension plans.

Points to watch The Ombudsman's decision is not binding – either on you or the society, so you can still take your case to court. At the time of writing, societies have (with one exception) so far complied with the Ombudsman's decisions, and if they didn't they would have to publicise their reasons for not doing so and include an explanation in their annual report. The Ombudsman has the power to make awards up to £100,000.

Office of the Building Societies Ombudsman
Grosvenor Gardens House, 35–37 Grosvenor Gardens,
London SW1X 7AW
Tel: 01-931 0044

Going to court

If you lose money because of the actions of an investment company or adviser, you could take them to court – for example, you might be able to sue them for negligence or misrepresentation. If Financial Services Act rules have been breached, you could bring a case under section 62 of the Act. But taking a financial institution through the courts would be a lengthy and, in most cases, costly exercise. You'd be wise to consider it only as a last resort after you've used other available complaints procedures. If you have a choice between going to court or giving up that right and using an arbitration service instead, consider getting some preliminary advice, for example from a Citizens Advice Bureau or a solicitor, before making your decision. Arbitration is usually cheaper and faster, but if the decision goes against you, you may regret having given up your right to court action.

Compensation

If you lose money through the fraud or negligence of an investment business and the company has gone bust, you may be able to get compensation through one of the schemes which apply to investments.

The SIB compensation scheme covers the first £30,000 of your investment in full and 90 per cent of the next £20,000 – giving maximum compensation of £48,000. If you think you have a claim against this scheme, contact the SIB (see p. 156).

Insurance-linked investments are covered by the older Policyholders' Protection Act scheme. This covers 90 per cent of your claim against the company with no upper limit at all. If you think you have a claim against this scheme, contact:

Policyholders' Protection Board
Aldermary House, Queen Street, London EC4N 1TT
Tel: 01-248 4477

Claims against banks, other than those covered by the Financial Services Act, may be covered by the compensation scheme set up under the Banking Act 1987. This covers up to 75 per cent of the first £20,000 of your deposits – maximum compensation of £15,000. If you think you have a claim against this scheme, contact:

Deposit Protection Board
19 Old Jewry, London EC2R 8HA
Tel: 01-601 5020

Claims against authorised building societies, other than those covered by the Financial Services Act, may be covered by the compensation scheme set up under the Building Societies Act 1986. This covers up to 90 per cent of the first £20,000 of your investment – maximum compensation of £18,000. If you think you have a claim against this scheme, contact:

Building Societies Investor Protection Board
15 Great Marlborough Street, London W1V 2AX
Tel: 01-437 9992

Some professions, such as solicitors and accountants, are covered by their own compensation schemes, as well as requiring members to have Professional Indemnity (PI) insurance which should ensure that the member is able to compensate you if you lost money through the firm's negligence or fraud.

Index

INDEX

INDEX

INDEX